Pink Lemonade
& Other Delights

10 Refreshing Quilt Projects

LINDA JOHNSON

& COMPANY

BOTHELL, WASHINGTON

Pink Lemonade and Other Delights: 10 Refreshing Quilt
Projects
© 2001 by Linda Johnson

That Patchwork Place is an imprint of Martingale & Company.
Martingale & Company
PO Box 118
Bothell, WA 98041-0118
www.martingale-pub.com

Printed in China
06 05 04 03 02 01   8 7 6 5 4 3 2 1

Library of Congress Cataloging-in-Publication Data
Johnson, Linda
      Pink lemonade and other delights: 10 refreshing quilt proj-
ects / Linda Johnson
         p. cm.
      ISBN 1-56477-324-8
      1. Patchwork—Patterns. 2. Appliqué—Patterns. 3. Quilts.
I. Title.

TT835 .J64 2001
746.46'041—dc21
                                                    00-063802

Mission Statement

We are dedicated to providing quality products and
service by working together to inspire creativity and
to enrich the lives we touch.

Credits

President · Nancy J. Martin
CEO · Daniel J. Martin
Publisher · Jane Hamada
Editorial Director · Mary V. Green
Editorial Project Manager · Tina Cook
Technical Editor · Darra Williamson
Copy Editor · Karen Koll
Design and Production Manager · Stan Green
Illustrator · Robin Strobel
Cover and Text Designer · Trina Stahl
Photographer · Brent Kane

Dedication

THIS BOOK IS dedicated to the memory of three great ladies: Elena Lundquist Rydquist, my grandmother; Iva Rydquist, my aunt; and Mabel Rydquist Erickson, my mother.

My grandmother was an adolescent when she came from Sweden with her family to settle in a sod house in Kansas. In the succeeding years, she married and had eight children, moving west to Washington State, then on to central California. My mother, the youngest child, remembers Grandma taking her five girls window shopping, then going home to make them each a favorite dress—without a pattern! Grandma also made quilts, but none of them has survived. I like to think this is because they comforted, warmed, and snuggled eight squirmy children in a slightly drafty old farmhouse. I never met my grandmother, but I have been told I'm a lot like her.

Aunt Iva and Uncle Roly lived in the same farmhouse as my grandparents. As a child, I would go to the farm for a week each summer. Cows, tractors, irrigation ditches, big, tall boots, and Swedish pancakes . . . I loved it! Aunt Iva taught me how to use the sewing machine when I was nine, and I've been sewing ever since.

Before marrying, my mother taught kindergarten through fourth grade in a two-room schoolhouse. She then helped my dad with his business for fifty years. Although she hated to sew, she loved that I liked to and encouraged me in my creative endeavors.

Acknowledgments

My thanks to
Mary Stanton for a timely introduction,
Kathy Bley for her quilting skills,
Irene Moss and Gale Roberson for technical assistance,
the Sew & Sews for their enthusiasm and encouragement,
and my family for their patience.

Contents

Preface

THIS BOOK BEGAN one hot day while I was lying on a raft in the middle of a small lake. As I drifted somewhere between a new quilt plan and sleep, I became aware of a slight touch on my eyebrow. I slowly opened my eyes to see two beautiful, bright blue dragonfly wings . . . and nothing more. Soon the dragonfly flew away. Now, I'm used to dragonflies landing on my toes or knees, but somehow this seemed just a tad more personal.

Instantly, that dragonfly became part of the quilt I was planning. Then a few more bugs arrived, but only good bugs! (I'm sure that insects were all good when God made them, but some—like the hornets, mosquitoes, and yellow jackets—hung out with the serpent in the Garden of Eden and got corrupted. So, I stick to the helpful ones.)

Enjoy!

General Instructions

Fabric

Select high-quality, 100 percent–cotton fabrics. Cotton fabrics hold their shape well and are easy to handle. Preshrink all fabric to test for colorfastness and to remove any excess dye. Place fabric in a sink or washing machine with tepid water and soak for ten minutes. Do not use soap or agitate. This method preserves the sizing in the fabric and keeps it from raveling. Run the washing machine through the spin cycle or gently hand wring the fabric to remove excess water. Dry in a dryer. Press the fabric so you can cut the pieces accurately.

All of the projects in this book are made using many different prints within each color range. For example, the thirty-two leaves in "Aphid Harvest" (page 61) are cut from seventeen different green prints. This variety gives the design more texture, depth, and visual interest. A large scrap bag will come in very handy, but working with ¼-yard cuts or trading small pieces with other quilters will also give you lots of alternatives. For these designs, more prints are definitely better!

Pattern and Perspective

No two flowers are exactly the same in nature, even on the same plant. So why should flowers on a quilt all be alike? You can give each flower a different look by combining the pattern pieces differently. You can even change the perspective from which you look at them. The flowers below are all created from the same pattern pieces, but each one seems to be facing a different way because of the way the pieces are layered and the stems positioned. Number 1 seems to be facing down and to the left, number 2 is facing straight forward, and number 3 is facing up and to the right.

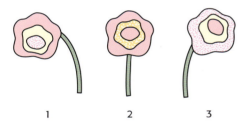

1   2   3

Rearrange the patterns to your heart's content: flip them over, turn them, change the colors. Make these patterns your own.

Supplies

Marking Tools: Various tools are available for tracing around templates or marking quilting lines. Use a water-erasable marker, a sharp No. 2 pencil, or fine-leaded mechanical pencil on light-colored fabrics, and a silver, white, or yellow marking pencil on dark fabrics. Chalk pencils or chalk-wheel markers also make clear marks on fabric. Be sure to test your marking tool to make sure you can remove its marks easily. For adding detail to appliqués, try a Sakura Pigma Micron pen or other permanent marker.

> *I use a paintbrush to erase markings made with a water-erasable marker. Try it! It works great.*

Needles: A size 70/10, 75/11, or 80/12 needle works well for machine piecing most cottons. For hand appliqué, choose a needle that glides easily through the edges of the appliqué pieces. Size 10 (fine) to size 12 (very fine) Sharp, Milliner, or straw needles work well, with length being a personal preference. Use a size 9 to size 12 Between needle for hand quilting, selecting the size that best suits your hand and gives you the best results.

Pins: Long, thin "quilter's" pins with glass or plastic heads are easy to handle.

Rotary-Cutting Tools: You'll need a rotary cutter, cutting mat, and clear acrylic rulers in a variety of sizes, including 6" x 6", 6" x 24", and 12" x 12".

Scissors: Reserve your best scissors to cut fabric only. Use an older pair of scissors to cut paper, cardboard, and template plastic. Small 4" scissors are handy for appliqué and clipping threads.

Seam Ripper: Use this tool to remove stitches from incorrectly sewn seams.

Sewing Machine: To machine piece, you'll need a sewing machine that has a good straight stitch. You'll also need a walking foot or darning foot if you are going to machine quilt.

Template Plastic: Use clear or frosted plastic (available at quilt shops) to make durable, accurate templates.

Thread: For piecing, use a good quality, all-purpose cotton thread. For appliqué, select a 60-weight, all-cotton machine embroidery thread or a 100-weight silk thread. Silk thread is my favorite because it sinks into the fabric and becomes almost invisible after stitching. In fact, a handful of colors work with almost any color fabric because the thread blends so well. However, it has a tendency to slip off the needle easily, so it is helpful to tie a tiny knot right next to the needle eye. This knot will pass through the fabric without any problems.

Machine Piecing

Sewing Accurate Seam Allowances

The most important thing to remember when machine piecing is to maintain a consistent ¼"-wide seam allowance. If you do not, the quilt blocks will not be the desired finished size, which in turn affects the size of everything else in the quilt, including alternate blocks, sashings, and borders.

Some machines have a special foot that measures exactly ¼" from the center needle position to the right edge of the foot. This feature allows you to use the edge of the presser foot to guide the fabric for a perfect ¼"-wide seam allowance.

If your machine doesn't have such a foot, create a seam guide by placing the edge of a piece of tape or moleskin ¼" to the right of the needle.

Pressing

The traditional rule in quiltmaking is to press seams to one side, toward the darker color wherever possible. Press the seam flat from the wrong side first, and then press the seam in the desired direction from the right side. Press carefully to avoid

distorting the shapes. Project illustrations include pressing arrows; press the seams in the direction of the arrows unless otherwise noted.

Plan ahead when joining two seamed units. Press the seam allowances in opposite directions as shown to reduce bulk and to make it easier to match seam lines. Pin through matched seam lines to hold them in place while stitching.

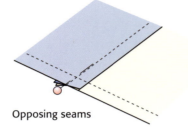

Opposing seams

Basic Appliqué

Instructions are provided here for needle-turn appliqué. Feel free to use another method if you prefer, adapting the templates and instructions as necessary.

Making Templates

Templates made from clear plastic are more durable and accurate than those made from cardboard. Since you can see through the plastic, it is easy to trace the patterns accurately.

Place template plastic over each pattern piece and trace with a fine-line permanent marker. Do not add seam allowances. Cut out the templates on the drawn lines. You need only one template for each different motif or shape. Mark the pattern name and grain-line arrow (if applicable) on the template.

Preparing the Background Fabric

Cut the background pieces the size and shape required for each project. Use the illustrations provided for the project, along with the photo of the quilt, as a model for positioning the appliqué pieces.

Needle-Turn Appliqué

Needle-turn appliqué moves directly from cutting to the appliqué stitch. You do not turn under and baste the seam allowances. The following steps describe the process.

1. Trace the appliqué design onto the right side of the appliqué fabric. Use a water-erasable marker to mark on light fabrics, and a silver, white, or yellow pencil when working with dark fabrics.

2. Cut out each fabric piece, adding a scant $\frac{1}{4}$"-wide seam allowance all around.

3. Refer to the appliqué placement diagram and position an appliqué piece on the background fabric. Pin or baste the appliqué in place.

4. Starting on a straight edge, use the tip of the needle to gently turn under the seam allowance, about $\frac{1}{2}$" at a time. Hold the turned seam allowance firmly between the thumb and first finger of your left hand (reverse if left-handed) as you stitch the appliqué to the background. Use a longer needle—a Sharp, Milliner, or straw

needle—to help you control the seam allowance and turn it under neatly. Use the traditional appliqué stitch (described below) to sew the appliqué pieces to the background.

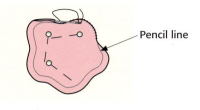

Pencil line

Traditional Appliqué Stitch

The traditional appliqué stitch, or blind stitch, is appropriate for sewing all appliqué shapes, including sharp points and curves. The following steps describe the process.

1. Tie a knot in a single strand of thread approximately 18" long.

2. Hide the knot by slipping the needle into the seam allowance from the wrong side of the appliqué piece, bringing it out on the fold line.

3. Work from right to left if you are right-handed, or left to right if you are left-handed. Start the first stitch by moving the needle straight off the appliqué, inserting the needle into the background fabric. Let the needle travel under the background fabric, parallel to the edge of the appliqué, bringing it up about $\frac{1}{8}$" away, along the traced line on the fold.

4. As you bring the needle up, pierce the folded edge of the appliqué piece, catching only 1 or 2 threads.

5. Move the needle straight off the appliqué into the background fabric, slightly under the appliqué piece. Let the needle travel under the

background, bringing it up about ⅛" away, again catching the folded edge of the appliqué.

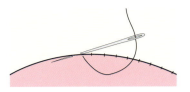

6. Give the thread a slight tug every 5 or 6 stitches and continue stitching.

7. To end your stitching, pull the needle through to the wrong side of the background fabric. Take two small stitches behind the appliqué piece, and make knots by taking your needle through the loops. Check the right side to see if the thread "shadows" through your background. If it does, take one more small stitch on the back side of the fabric to direct the tail of the thread under the appliqué fabric.

8. If desired, trim the background fabric behind each appliqué piece to eliminate shadow-through, reduce bulk, and make it easier to quilt. Turn the block over and make a tiny cut in the background fabric behind the appliqué. Trim the background fabric inside the stitching line, leaving a ¼" seam allowance. Be careful not to cut into the appliqué piece.

Wrong side of background fabric

Use the tip of your needle to manipulate the seam allowance of the appliqué piece as needed to maintain a straight edge or smooth curve. If necessary, clip into the seam allowance of an inside curve or point to prevent tension or puckering.

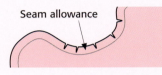

Seam allowance

As you stitch toward a sharp outside point, start taking smaller stitches within ½" of the point. Trim the seam allowance and push the excess fabric under the point with the tip of your needle. If there is still some bulkiness after the point has been stitched, rub the point between your thumb and forefinger. That should help distribute the bulk evenly.

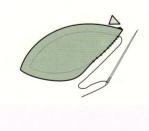

Cutting Bias Strips for Appliqué

Cut fabric as directed in the specific project instructions. Use your rotary cutter and clear acrylic ruler to cut the fabric into strips along the bias of the fabric in the width (or widths) described in the cutting instructions.

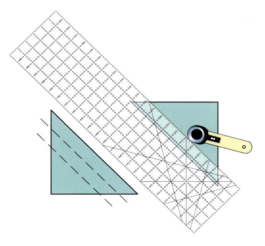

Making "Bugs"

Many of the projects in this book feature fanciful insects. The following instructions describe the basic procedures for making them. Individual project instructions will tell you which and how many to make and where to place them. Refer to "Basic Appliqué" (pages 8–11) and "Basic Embroidery Stitches" (page 14) for guidance as needed.

Dragonflies

1. Use the pattern below to make a template for the dragonfly wings. Trace and cut wings from the appropriate appliqué fabric, adding a scant ¼" seam allowance around the traced lines as you cut.

Dragonfly wings pattern

2. Refer to the appliqué placement diagram given for the specific project. Appliqué the wings, with their centers touching, to the background fabric.

3. Cut one 2⅜" x ⅞" bias strip. Fold the strip in half lengthwise and press. Place the strip over the wings as shown, with the top edge extending ⅜" beyond the top of the wings and the tail end slightly curved to one side.

4. Machine stitch ¼" from the raw edge, stopping ³⁄₁₆" from each end. Trim the seam allowance to ⅛".

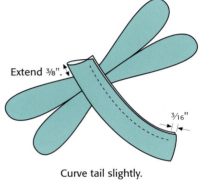

Extend ⅜".

³⁄₁₆"

Curve tail slightly.

5. Turn the pressed folded edge to cover the trimmed seam allowance. Appliqué the folded edge by hand, tucking in and stitching the two short edges to finish.

6. Use 2 strands of embroidery floss to make French-knot eyes.

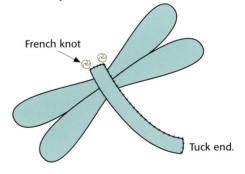

French knot

Tuck end.

Hand appliqué folded edge.

Ladybugs

These can be made ahead and set aside until you are ready to appliqué them onto the quilt top.

My favorite method for making perfect appliqué circle patterns was inspired by quiltmaker Linda Brannock. Place a plastic architect's circle template (available at office supply stores) on top of an old magazine cover and continue tracing inside the template with a ballpoint pen until the paper circle pops out. Use the $^{15}/_{32}$" size template for the ladybugs in this book.

1. Use an architect's template as described above or use the pattern below to make 1 paper pattern for each ladybug required for your specific project. Do not add seam allowances.

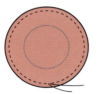

Ladybug pattern

2. Use the same ladybug template to trace a circle of red fabric for each ladybug. Cut out the fabric circle, adding a scant $^{1}/_{4}$" seam allowance around the traced line as you cut. Run a basting stitch around the perimeter of the fabric circle inside the seam allowance. Do not pull the basting stitches tight.

3. Center a paper circle pattern on the wrong side of each fabric circle. Pull the basting stitches to gather the excess fabric around the paper pattern into a nice, smooth circle. Use a needle or pin to smooth curves if necessary. Tie the thread ends securely.

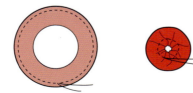

4. Spray the stitched and gathered circle thoroughly with spray starch and press both sides with an iron until flat and dry.

5. When you are ready to appliqué the ladybugs, remove the gathering stitches and paper templates. The starch will keep the edge crisp as you sew the appliqués in place.

6. Use a black Pigma pen to put heads, wings, dots, and other markings on your bugs.

Bees

Note: *If you use an architect's plastic template to make the paper patterns as described for ladybugs, select a $^{15}/_{32}$" ellipse template rather than a circle.*

1. Use an architect's template as described above or use the pattern below to make a bee body template. Trace the template to make 1 paper pattern for each bee required for your specific project. Do not add seam allowances.

Bee body pattern

2. Use the same ellipse template to trace an oval of tan fabric with black stripes for each bee, carefully positioning the template so that the stripes are properly placed on the bee's body. Cut out the fabric oval, adding a scant $^{1}/_{4}$" seam allowance around the traced line as you cut. Run a basting stitch around the perimeter of the fabric oval, inside the seam allowance. Do not pull the stitches tight.

3. Center a paper pattern on the wrong side of each fabric oval. Pull the basting stitches to gather the excess fabric around the paper

pattern. Use a needle or pin to smooth curves; tie thread ends securely.

4. Spray the stitched and gathered oval thoroughly with spray starch and press both sides with an iron until flat and dry.

> *Don't worry if you can't find the perfect striped fabric for bee bodies. Stripes can be added to solid fabric bodies with a black Pigma pen after the appliqué has been starched and pressed.*
>
>

5. Use the pattern below to make templates for the bee wings. Trace and cut 2 wings for each bee from the appropriate appliqué fabric, adding a scant ¼" seam allowance around the traced lines as you cut.

Bee wing pattern

6. Refer to the appliqué placement diagram given for the specific project. Appliqué the curved edges of the wings to the background fabric. The wings may be appliquéd in either of the positions shown below.

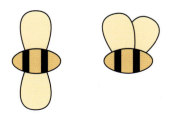

You do not need to appliqué the short, straight edges of the wings, as the bee's body will cover them.

7. Just before appliquéing the bee's body, remove the gathering stitches and paper pattern. Appliqué the bee's body in place, making sure to cover the raw edges of the wings.

Spider and Web

1. Transfer the spiderweb pattern for your project to the background fabric. With 1 strand of gray floss, use the backstitch (page 14) to embroider the spiderweb onto the background fabric.

2. Refer to "Ladybugs," steps 1 through 5, on page 12 and use black fabric to make the spider bodies.

3. Refer to the appliqué placement diagram given for the specific project to appliqué the spider body onto the web.

4. Use 2 strands of black embroidery floss and the satin stitch (page 14) to embroider a small head onto the spider.

5. Use 1 strand of black embroidery floss and the backstitch (page 14) to embroider 8 legs on the spider.

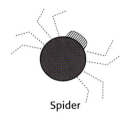

Spider

Basic Embroidery Stitches

Many of the projects in this book use basic embroidery stitches to add realism and whimsy. Refer to the following diagrams for assistance in creating these embroidered details.

Backstitch

Satin Stitch

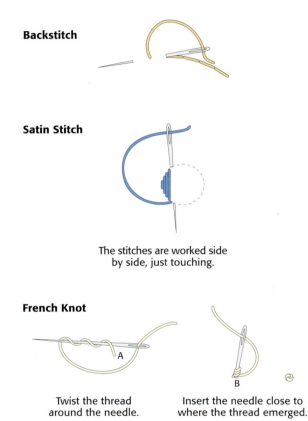

The stitches are worked side by side, just touching.

French Knot

Twist the thread around the needle.

Insert the needle close to where the thread emerged.

Note: *Wrap thread once, twice, or three times around needle depending on size of knot desired.*

Feather Stitch

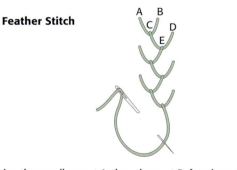

Bring the needle up at A, then down at B, forming a U shape.
Bring the needle back up at C to form the "catch,"
then down at D, once again forming a U shape.

Assembling the Quilt Top

Squaring Up Blocks

When your blocks are complete, take the time to square them up. Use a large square ruler to measure your blocks and make sure they are the desired size, plus an exact ¼" on each edge for seam allowances. For example, if you are making 6" blocks, they should all measure 6½" x 6½" before you sew them together. If your blocks vary slightly in size, trim the larger blocks to match the size of the smallest one. Be sure to trim all four sides; otherwise, your block will be lopsided.

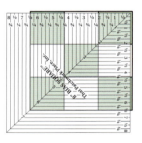

If your blocks are not the required finished size, you will have to adjust all the other components of the quilt accordingly.

Straight-Cut Borders

1. Measure the length of the quilt top through the center. Cut 2 border strips to that measurement, piecing as necessary. Mark the center of the quilt edges and the border strips. Pin the borders to the sides of the quilt top, matching the center marks and ends and easing as necessary. Sew the border strips in place. Press seams toward the border.

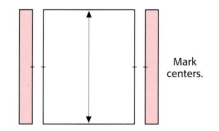

Mark centers.

Measure center of quilt, top to bottom.

2. Measure the width of the quilt top through the center, including the side borders just added. Cut 2 border strips to that measurement, piecing as necessary. Mark the center of the quilt edges and the border strips. Pin the borders to the top and bottom edges of the quilt top, matching the center marks and ends and easing as necessary; stitch. Press seams toward the border.

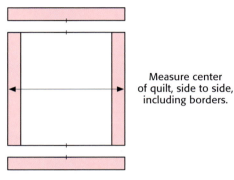

Measure center of quilt, side to side, including borders.

Mark centers.

Preparing the Quilt

Marking the Quilting Lines

Whether or not to mark the quilting designs depends upon the type of quilting you will be doing. Marking is not necessary if you plan to quilt in the ditch, outline-quilt a uniform distance from seam lines, or free-motion quilt by machine in a random pattern. For more complex quilting designs, however, you'll want to mark the quilt top before the quilt is layered with batting and backing.

Choose a marking tool that will be visible on your fabric and test it on fabric scraps to be sure the marks can be removed easily. See "Marking Tools" on page 7 for options. You can also use masking tape to mark straight quilting. Tape only small sections at a time and remove the tape when you stop at the end of the day; otherwise, the sticky residue may be difficult to remove from the fabric.

Layering the Quilt

The quilt "sandwich" consists of the backing, batting, and quilt top. Cut the quilt backing at least 4" larger than the quilt top all the way around. For large quilts, it is usually necessary to sew two or three lengths of fabric together to make a backing the required size. Trim away the selvages before piecing the lengths together. Press the backing seams open to make quilting easier.

Batting comes packaged in standard bed sizes, or it can be purchased by the yard. Several weights or thicknesses are available. A thinner batting is best if you intend to quilt by hand or machine. A thicker batting can be used if you will be tying your quilt.

To put the quilt sandwich together:

1. Spread the backing, wrong side up, on a flat, clean surface. Anchor it with pins or masking tape. Keep the backing taut, but be careful not to stretch it out of shape.

2. Spread the batting over the backing, smoothing out any wrinkles.

3. Center the pressed quilt top, right side up, on top of the batting. Smooth out any wrinkles and make sure the edges of the quilt top are parallel to the edges of the backing.

4. Starting in the center, baste with needle and thread and work diagonally to each corner. Continue basting in a grid of horizontal and vertical

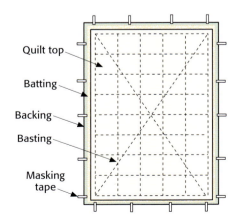

Quilt top

Batting

Backing

Basting

Masking tape

lines 6" to 8" apart. Finish by basting around the edges. Trim any excess backing or batting to within 3" of the quilt top.

Note: *For machine quilting, you may baste the layers of the quilt sandwich with #1 rustproof safety pins. Place pins about 6" to 8" apart, away from the areas you intend to quilt.*

Quilting Techniques

Hand Quilting

To quilt by hand, you will need short, sturdy needles (called "Betweens"), quilting thread, and a thimble to fit the middle finger of your sewing hand. Most quilters also use a frame or hoop to support their work. Use the smallest needle you can comfortably handle; the finer the needle, the smaller your stitches will be.

1. Thread your needle with a single strand of quilting thread about 18" long. Make a small knot and insert the needle in the top layer about 1" from the place where you want to start stitching. Pull the needle out at the point where quilting will begin and gently pull the thread until the knot pops through the fabric and into the batting.

2. Begin with a small backstitch and then make small, evenly spaced stitches through all 3 layers. Rock the needle up and down through all layers until you have 3 or 4 stitches on the needle. Place your other hand underneath the quilt so you can feel the needle point with the tip of your finger when a stitch is taken.

3. To end a line of quilting, make a small knot close to the last stitch; then backstitch, running the thread a needle's length through the batting.

Gently pull the thread until the knot pops into the batting. Clip the thread at the quilt's surface.

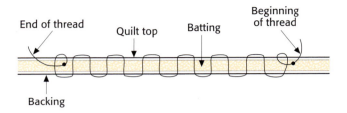

Machine Quilting

Machine quilting is suitable for all types of quilts, from crib-size to full-size bed quilts. With machine quilting, you can quickly complete quilts that might otherwise languish on the shelf.

For straight-line quilting, you need a walking foot to help feed the quilt layers through the machine without shifting or puckering. Some machines have a built-in walking foot; other machines require a separate attachment.

For free-motion quilting, you need a darning foot and the ability to drop the feed dogs on your machine. With free-motion quilting, you do not turn the fabric under the needle but instead guide the fabric in the direction of the design. Use free-motion quilting to outline-quilt a pattern in the fabric or to create stippling or other curved designs.

Finishing

Binding

Straight strips cut across the width of the fabric can be used on straight-sided quilts, but I prefer bias binding on all quilts. I find it is easier to work with and wears longer. For a French double-fold binding, cut bias strips to the width given with the specific project instructions, usually 2½" to 2¾". You will need enough strips to go around the perimeter of the quilt, plus 15" for seams and the corners in a mitered fold.

1. Align the 45° marking of your long acrylic ruler with the left edge of the fabric you have designated for the binding. Cut strips of the desired width from the diagonal (bias) of the fabric.

   Note: *If you are left-handed, align the 45° marking of your ruler with the* right *edge of the fabric.*

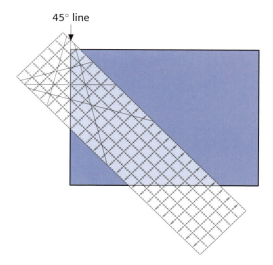

45° line

2. With right sides together, join strips as shown to make 1 long piece of binding. Press seams open.

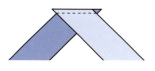

3. Fold the strip in half lengthwise, wrong sides together, and press.

Fold line

4. Align the raw edges of the binding with the raw edges of the quilt top. Starting 10" from the end of the bias binding strip, in the middle of one side of the quilt, use a ¼"-wide seam allowance and your walking foot to stitch the binding to the quilt. End the stitching ¼" from the corner of the quilt and backstitch.

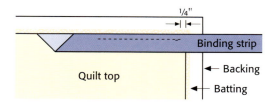

¼"

Binding strip

Quilt top

Backing

Batting

5. Turn the quilt so that you'll be stitching down the next side. Fold the binding up, away from the quilt, with raw edges aligned. Fold the binding back down onto itself, even with the edge of the quilt top. Begin stitching at the edge, backstitching to secure. Repeat on the remaining edges and corners of the quilt.

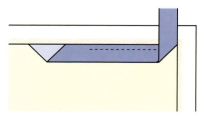

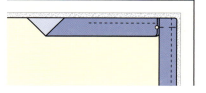

6. Stop stitching approximately 15" from the point at which you started. Halfway between the starting and stopping points, cut the end of 1 bias strip at a 45° angle. Unfold both bias strips and lay the cut strip on top of the uncut bias strip. Cut the bottom bias strip at a 45° angle so that the 2 bias strips overlap by ½" and the angles are both cut in the same direction.

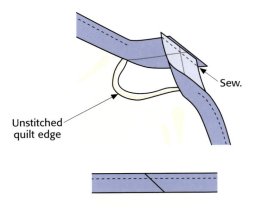

7. Stitch the 2 ends right sides together as in step 2. Press the seam open and refold the binding. The connected binding should be the right length to fit between the stopping and starting points of your stitching. Stitch between the starting and stopping points.

8. Trim the excess batting and backing to ½" beyond the stitching line.

9. Fold the binding over the raw edges of the quilt to the back, with the folded edge covering the row of machine stitching. Blindstitch the binding in place. A miter will form at each corner. Blindstitch the mitered corners.

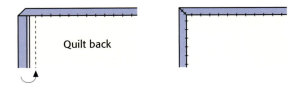

Adding a Sleeve

If you plan to display your finished quilt on a wall, be sure to include a hanging sleeve to hold the rod.

1. Using leftover fabric from the front or the back of the quilt (or a piece of muslin), cut a strip 6" to 8" wide by the width of the quilt at the top edge, minus 1". Fold the short ends under ½", then ½" again; stitch.

2. Fold the fabric strip in half lengthwise, wrong sides together, and stitch the long raw edge with a ¼" seam. Center the seam and press.

3. Position the sleeve just below the binding, along the top edge of the quilt back. Be sure the seam is turned toward the quilt. Blindstitch the top and bottom edges of the sleeve in place. Push the bottom edge of the sleeve up just a bit to provide a little give so the hanging rod does not put strain on the quilt itself.

Signing Your Quilt

Be sure to sign and date your quilt. Future generations will want to know more than just who made your quilt and when. Labels can be as elaborate or as simple as you desire. You can write, type, or embroider the information. Be sure to include your name, the name of the quilt, your city and state, the date, the name of the recipient if it is a gift, and any other interesting or important information about the quilt.

Pink Lemonade

PINK LEMONADE by Linda Johnson, 1999, Auburn, Washington, 87¾" x 87¾".

Hand quilted by Miller's Dry Goods.

*T*his is the quilt I was planning when I was gently accosted by a dragonfly
(see "Preface" on page 5). He instantly became a part of the center and border of this quilt . . .
but he looked lonely, so a few of his friends joined him.

You can enhance the scrappiness of this quilt by using as many pink, yellow, and green fabrics as
possible, and by varying the placement and number of leaves on each stem.

This quilt was inspired in part by the quilt "Buttermilk Farm" by Teri Christopherson.

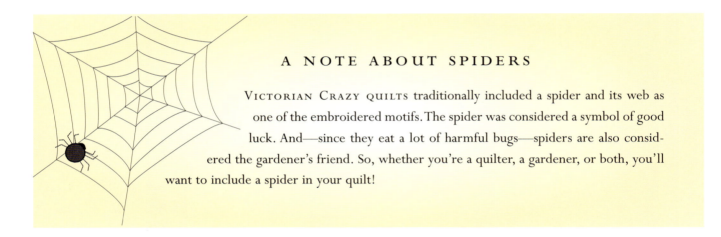

A NOTE ABOUT SPIDERS

VICTORIAN CRAZY QUILTS traditionally included a spider and its web as
one of the embroidered motifs. The spider was considered a symbol of good
luck. And—since they eat a lot of harmful bugs—spiders are also considered the gardener's friend. So, whether you're a quilter, a gardener, or both, you'll
want to include a spider in your quilt!

FINISHED QUILT SIZE: 87¾" x 87¾"
FINISHED BLOCK SIZE: 6¼"

Materials
42"-wide fabric

- 1⅛ yds. medium yellow print fabric for Hourglass blocks
- 1⅜ yds. medium pink print for Hourglass blocks
- 1¾ yds. *total* of assorted pink prints for Irish Chain blocks and flower appliqués

- 2½ yds. *total* of assorted yellow prints for Irish Chain blocks and flower appliqués
- 2½ yds. *total* of assorted green prints for vines and leaves
- 3⅜ yds. muslin for center appliqué background and outer border
- 1⅜ yds. dark pink print for inner borders and bias binding
- Purple and blue scraps for dragonfly and dragonfly wing appliqués
- Tan/black stripe scraps for bee appliqués
- Light tan scraps for bee wing appliqués
- Red scraps for ladybug appliqués

- Black scraps for spider appliqués
- 8 yds. fabric for backing
- 90" x 90" piece of batting
- Gray, black, and yellow embroidery floss
- Architect's plastic circle and ellipse templates
- Black Pigma pen

Cutting

All cutting measurements include ¼"-wide seam allowances.

From the medium yellow print, cut:
- 5 strips, each 7½" x 42", for Hourglass blocks. Crosscut strips into 25 squares, each 7½" x 7½".

From the medium pink print, cut:
- 6 strips, each 7½" x 42", for Hourglass blocks. Crosscut strips into 26 squares, each 7½" x 7½".

From the assorted pink prints, cut a *total* of:
- 20 strips, each 1¾" x 42", for Irish Chain blocks. Crosscut the strips into a total of 468 squares, each 1¾" x 1¾".

From the assorted yellow prints, cut a *total* of:
- 31 strips, each 1¾" x 42", for Irish Chain blocks. Crosscut the strips into a total of 208 rectangles, each 1¾" x 4¼", and 208 squares, each 1¾" x 1¾".

One-eighth yard of fabric yields enough yellow pieces for 3 blocks, or enough pink pieces for 5 blocks.

From the muslin, cut:
- 1 square, 25¼" x 25¼", for center appliqué background
- 2 strips, each 9" x 87¾", from the *length* of the fabric, for outer border
- 2 strips, each 9" x 70¾", from the *length* of the fabric, for outer border

From the dark pink print, cut:
- 2 strips, each 1¼" x 25¼", for first inner border
- 2 strips, each 1¼" x 26¾", for first inner border
- 8 strips, each 1¼" x 42", for second inner border

Note: *Refer to "General Instructions" (pages 6–18) as needed for guidance with all basic construction techniques.*

Making the Pieced Blocks

You'll need 36 full Hourglass blocks, 28 partial Hourglass blocks (double-triangle units A and B), and 52 Irish Chain blocks for this quilt. All of the Hourglass blocks are made from 1 pink and 1 yellow print. The Irish Chain blocks are scrappy, and each uses nine 1¾" pink squares, four 1¾" yellow squares, and four 1¾" x 4¼" yellow rectangles.

Hourglass Blocks

1. Use a pencil to draw diagonal lines from corner to corner in both directions on the wrong side of each 7½" yellow square.

2. Pair each marked 7½" yellow square with a 7½" pink square, right sides together. Stitch ¼" from both sides of 1 diagonal line.

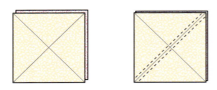

Note: *You'll have 1 pink square left over. Set it aside for now.*

3. Cut the unstitched line first, then cut the line between the rows of stitching. Unfold the pieces and press seams toward the pink triangles. You will have 100 double-triangle units: 50 each of Unit A and Unit B.

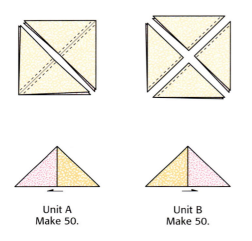

Unit A
Make 50.

Unit B
Make 50.

4. With right sides together and pinning carefully to match center seams, sew 2 identical double-triangle units together to make an Hourglass block. Press seams to one side. Make 36. Set the remaining double triangle units (14 each of A and B) aside for now.

Hourglass block
Make 36.

Irish Chain Blocks

1. Arrange five 1¾" pink squares and four 1¾" yellow squares in 3 rows as shown. Sew the squares into rows. Press seams toward the pink squares.

2. Pinning carefully to match seams, sew the rows together to make a nine-patch unit. Press seams in one direction.

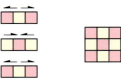

3. Sew a 1¾" x 4¼" yellow rectangle to opposite sides of the nine-patch unit. Press seams toward the rectangles.

4. Sew a 1¾" pink square to the short ends of a 1¾" x 4¼" yellow rectangle. Press seams toward the rectangles. Make 2.

5. Sew the unit from step 3 between the 2 units from step 4. Press seams away from the center unit.

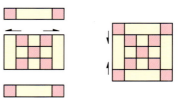

6. Repeat steps 1–5 to make a total of 52 blocks.

Preparing for Appliqué

1. From the assorted green prints, cut ⅞"-wide bias strips to total 300" for appliqué vines and vine stems.

If you prefer, you may cut all vines and stems from a single fabric. One-third yard of fabric will yield the necessary 300" length.

2. Sew the ⅞"-wide bias strips to make 1 continuous strip. Set aside for now.

3. Use the patterns on page 27 to make templates for the 2 extra-large, 3 large, and 3 medium flowers, the 2 flower centers, and the flower bud. You may use the flowers and flower centers in any combination. (You many pair any extra-large flower with any large flower, any medium flower, and any flower center.) Trace the templates and cut a total of 15 extra-large flowers, 20 large flowers, 15 medium flowers, 20 flower centers, and 12 flower buds from the remaining pink prints. Trace the templates and cut a total of 15 large flowers, 20 medium flowers, and 15 flower centers from the remaining yellow prints. Add a scant ¼" seam allowance to each fabric shape.

4. Use the patterns on page 27 to make templates for the leaves and bud cups. Trace the templates and cut a total of 212 leaves and 12 bud cups from the remaining green fabrics.

   Note: *Some of the leaves will be used as greenery behind the flowers.*

Appliquéing the Center Square

1. Fold the 25¼" muslin square in quarters to find its center, and then crease the block on both diagonals. These fold lines will assist you in centering the appliqué design on the background fabric.

2. Refer to the block appliqué placement diagram on page 24 and the photo on page 19. Lay out and pin the following pieces to form the center flower cluster on the muslin block: 4 short lengths of bias stem (cut from bias strip stitched previously), 4 green bud cups, 4 pink flower buds, 3 extra-large pink flowers, 3 large yellow flowers, 3 medium pink flowers, and 3 yellow flower centers. Add 3 green leaves to each center stem as shown, and tuck an additional 13 leaves as greenery around the flower cluster.

3. Appliqué the pieces in this order to the background block: bias stems, flower buds, bud cups, stem leaves, greenery leaves, extra-large flowers, large flowers, medium flowers, and flower centers. Trim leaves under flowers to reduce bulk.

4. Referring again to the placement diagram and photo, lay out and pin the following pieces to form the 4 "floating" flowers: 4 large pink flowers, 4 medium yellow flowers, and 4 pink flower centers. Tuck 2 or 3 leaves as greenery behind each flower as shown.

5. Appliqué the pieces in this order to the background block: leaves, large flowers, medium flowers, and flower centers. Trim leaves under flowers to reduce bulk. Set the remaining flower and leaf pieces aside for now.

6. Refer to the block appliqué placement diagram and use the purple and blue scraps to make and appliqué 1 dragonfly to the muslin block. Use

the yellow embroidery floss to add eyes. Use the tan/black stripe and light tan scraps to make and appliqué 1 bee. Use the red scraps and Pigma pen to make 1 ladybug. Appliqué the ladybug to a leaf as shown.

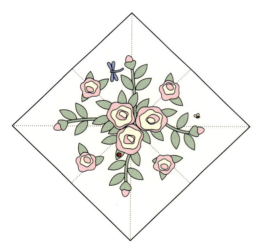

Block appliqué placement

Assembly

1. With right sides together, and matching center points and ends, sew a 1¼" x 25¼" dark pink first inner border strip to opposite sides of the appliquéd center square. Press seams toward the border strips.

2. Repeat to sew the 1¼" x 26¾" dark pink first inner border strips to the remaining sides of the center square. Press.

3. Cut the remaining 7½" pink square in half on both diagonals. Referring to the assembly diagram below, arrange 10 Irish Chain blocks, 6 full Hourglass blocks, 3 double-triangle A units, 3 double-triangle B units, and 2 quarter-square triangles in horizontal rows as shown in the upper left section of the assembly diagram.

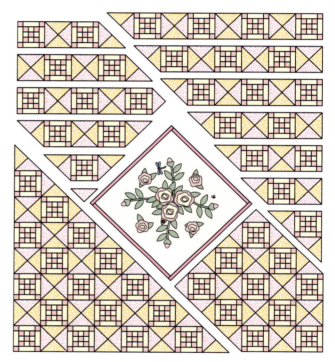

Assembly diagram

Take extra care when handling the double-triangle units so as not to stretch their long bias edges.

4. Sew the blocks, units, and triangles together into rows. Press seams in opposite directions from row to row.

5. With right sides together, and pinning carefully to match seams, sew the rows together. Press seams in one direction. Repeat steps 1–5 to make another unit.

6. Arrange 16 Irish Chain blocks, 12 full Hourglass blocks, 4 double-triangle A units, and 4 double-triangle B units in horizontal rows as shown in the upper right section of the assembly diagram on page 24.

7. Sew the blocks and units together into rows. Press seams in opposite directions from row to row.

8. With right sides together, and pinning carefully to match seams, sew the rows together. Press seams in one direction. Repeat steps 6–8 to make another unit.

9. Turn the bordered center block on-point. Referring to the assembly diagram, sew the units from step 5 to the upper left and lower right sides of the center block. Press seams toward the center block. Repeat to sew the units from step 8 to the remaining 2 sides of the center block. Press.

10. Sew the 1¼" x 42" dark pink second inner border strips together to make 1 continuous 1¼"-wide strip. Refer to "Straight-Cut Borders" on pages 14–15. Measure the quilt as directed, and cut the border strips from this 1¼"-wide strip. Sew the strips first to the sides, then to the top and bottom, and press.

Appliquéing the Outer Border

1. Refer to the border appliqué placement diagram and photo below. Lay out and pin the following pieces to each 9" x 70¾" outer border strip: 2 long lengths of curving vine, 2 pink flower buds, 2 bud cups, 4 short bias stems, 4 large pink flowers, 4 medium yellow flowers, 4 pink flower centers, and approximately 38 green leaves.

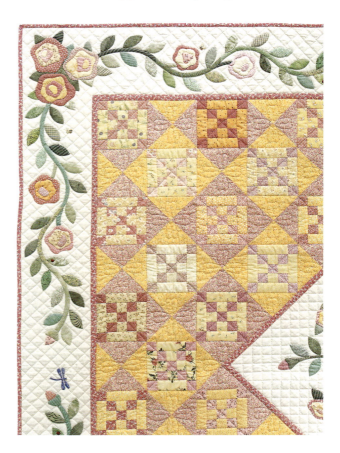

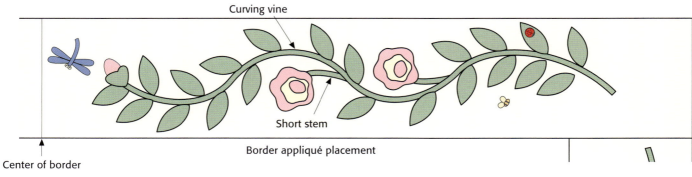

Curving vine

Short stem

Border appliqué placement

Center of border

2. Appliqué the pieces in this order to the border strip: short bias stems, curving vine, flower buds, bud cups, large flowers, medium flowers, flower centers, and leaves.

3. Refer to the border appliqué placement diagram and use the remaining blue and purple scraps to make and appliqué 1 dragonfly to each border strip. Add eyes with yellow embroidery floss. Use the remaining red scraps and Pigma pen to make and appliqué 2 ladybugs to each strip. Use the tan/black stripe and tan scraps to make and appliqué 2 bees to each strip.

4. Repeat steps 1 through 3 to lay out and appliqué the two 9" x 87¾" border strips. Be sure to leave the ends (corners) free from appliqué. The ends of the vines will be covered with flower clusters, and the appliqué corners completed, after the borders have been sewn to the quilt.

5. Sew the 9" x 70¾" outer border strips to the sides of the quilt and the 9" x 87¾" outer border strips to the top and bottom. Press.

6. Refer to the corner appliqué placement diagram below and the photo above right. Center 3 extra-large pink flowers, 3 large yellow flowers, 3 medium pink flowers, and 3 yellow flower centers over each corner of the border. Tuck an additional 8 to 10 leaves around each flower cluster as greenery. Make sure the cluster covers the vine "tails" on each adjacent border. Appliqué the pieces in place.

7. Trace the spiderweb pattern on page 27 onto 1 of the appliquéd borders, near a corner. Use gray embroidery floss and a backstitch to embroider the web. Use the black fabric scraps and black embroidery floss to make and appliqué a spider to the web.

Layering and Finishing

1. Divide the backing fabric crosswise into 3 equal panels of approximately 93" each. Remove the selvages and join the pieces to make a single, large backing panel.

2. Center and layer the quilt top and batting over the backing; baste.

3. Quilt as desired.

4. Use the remaining dark pink print to cut a total of 370" of 2¾"-wide bias binding strips. Sew the binding to the quilt.

5. Make a label and attach it to your quilt.

Curving vine

Corner appliqué placement

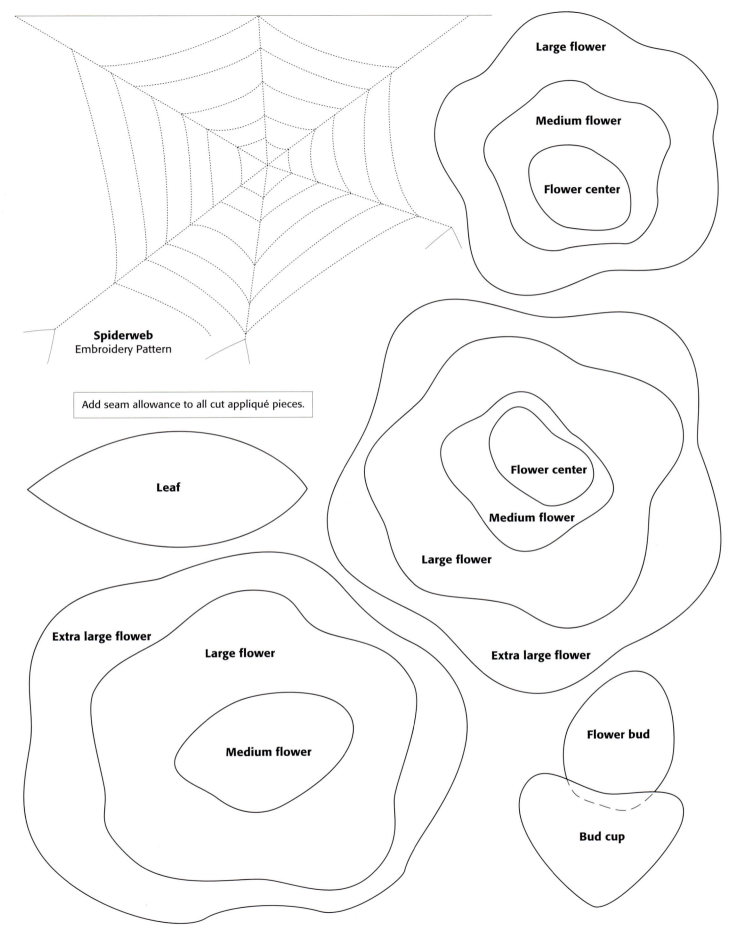

Spiderweb
Embroidery Pattern

Large flower

Medium flower

Flower center

Add seam allowance to all cut appliqué pieces.

Leaf

Flower center

Medium flower

Large flower

Extra large flower

Extra large flower

Large flower

Medium flower

Flower bud

Bud cup

Day and Night

DAY AND NIGHT by Linda Johnson, 1999, Auburn, Washington, 79" x 79".

Hand quilted by Kathy Bley.

This is a very noisy quilt! During the day the bees buzz loudly; you can see them on the quilt. And at night you can hear one of my favorite sounds: frogs. I love it when the frogs are waking up in spring. There is a place in my backyard where I get stereo frog surround-sound from two ponds and a ditch. If you close your eyes and listen really carefully, you can hear those same frog and cricket sounds coming from your quilt . . . but you can't see them, because it's dark!

A NOTE ABOUT HONEYBEES

HONEYBEES ARE VERY social insects. Each member of the colony has its own task to perform, and does it well. Hence we have the saying, "busy as a bee." In the end, we are the ones who reap the benefits of all their hard work—delicious honey. And don't forget the quilting bee!

FINISHED QUILT SIZE: 79" x 79"
FINISHED BLOCK SIZE: 7½"

Materials
42"-wide fabric

- 1⅛ yds. *total* of assorted dark floral prints for Nine Patch blocks
- 1 yd. *total* of assorted light floral prints for Nine Patch blocks
- 1¼ yds. pale yellow plaid for setting squares
- ½ yd. *total* of assorted light green fabrics for "day" leaf and vine appliqués
- ½ yd. *total* of assorted light pink, medium pink, and burgundy fabrics for flower appliqués

- ¼ yd. *total* of assorted yellow and gold fabrics for flower appliqués
- ⅜ yd. *total* of assorted dark green fabrics for "night" leaf and vine appliqués
- 3 yds. tone-on-tone black print for setting triangles and border
- Tan/black stripe scraps for bee appliqués
- Light tan scraps for bee wing appliqués
- 1 yd. fabric for bias binding
- 4¾ yds. fabric for backing
- 83" x 83" piece of batting
- Erasable marker
- Architect's plastic ellipse template
- Black Pigma pen

Cutting

All cutting measurements include ¼"-wide seam allowances.

From the assorted dark floral prints, cut a *total* of:

- 13 strips, each 3" x 42", for Nine Patch blocks. Crosscut strips into 180 squares, each 3" x 3".

From the assorted light floral prints, cut a *total* of:

- 11 strips, each 3" x 42", for Nine Patch blocks. Crosscut strips into 144 squares, each 3" x 3".

From the pale yellow plaid, cut:

- Five strips, each 8" x 42", for setting squares. Crosscut strips into 25 squares, each 8" x 8".

From the tone-on-tone black print, cut:

- 4 border pieces from the *length* of the fabric. Use the pattern on page 34.
- 5 squares, each 12" x 12", for side setting triangles. Cut squares twice diagonally to make 20 triangles.
- 2 squares, each 6½" x 6½", for corner setting triangles. Cut squares once diagonally to make 4 triangles.

    Note: *Refer to "General Instructions" (pages 6–18) as needed for guidance with all basic construction techniques.*

Nine Patch Blocks

You'll need 36 Nine Patch blocks for this quilt. You may make each block as scrappy as you wish. Each block uses five 3" dark floral squares and four 3" light floral squares. I chose to use 1 dark print and 1 light print in each square.

1. Arrange five 3" dark squares and four 3" light squares in 3 rows as shown. Sew the squares into rows. Press seams toward the dark squares.

2. Pinning carefully to match seams, sew the rows together to make a block. Press seams in one direction. Make 36.

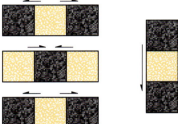 

Make 36.

Appliquéing the Center Squares

Note: *Refer to the appliqué placement diagrams on page 31 and the photo on page 28 when positioning appliqués.*

1. Fold a pale yellow 8" square in quarters to find its center, and then crease the block on both diagonals. Repeat for 4 additional 8" blocks. These fold lines will assist you in centering the appliqué designs on the background fabric.

2. Use the patterns on page 34 to make templates for pattern pieces A–D. Trace the templates and cut 7 A pieces from the assorted light green prints, 3 each of pieces B and D from the assorted light and medium pink fabrics, and 3 C pieces from the assorted yellow fabrics. Add a scant ¼" seam allowance to each fabric shape.

3. Refer to center square placement diagram on page 31. Position and pin the appliqués on a creased background square, tucking the 7 leaves behind the flower cluster as greenery. Appliqué

the pieces in this order to the background block: 7 A, 3 B, 3 C, and 3 D. Trim leaves and under flowers to reduce bulk.

Center square appliqué placement

4. Use the patterns on page 34 to make templates for pattern pieces E–G. Trace the templates and cut 8 A pieces from the assorted light green prints, 4 each of pieces E and G from matching light and medium pink fabrics, and 4 F pieces from the assorted yellow fabrics. Add a scant ¼" seam allowance to each fabric shape.

5. Position and pin the appliqués on the 4 remaining creased background squares, tucking 2 leaves behind each flower as shown. Appliqué the pieces in this order to each background block: 2 A, 1 E, 1 F, and 1 G.

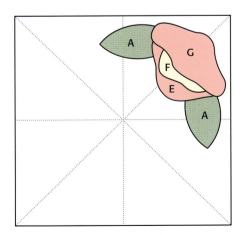

Outer square appliqué placement

Appliquéing the Setting Squares and Triangles

Note: *Refer to the appliqué placement diagrams and the photo on page 28 when positioning appliqués.*

1. Fold eight 8" pale yellow squares as described in "Appliquéing the Center Squares," step 1, on page 30.

2. Cut a total of 8 bias strips, each ⅞" x 10", from the various light green prints, and a total of 12 bias strips, each ⅞" x 10", from the dark green prints for the appliqué vines. Set aside for now.

3. Trace the templates and cut 10 A pieces from the assorted light green prints, 5 each of pieces E and G from matching light and medium pink fabrics, and 5 F pieces from the assorted yellow fabrics. Add a scant ¼" seam allowance to each fabric shape.

4. Position and pin the appliqués and strips of light green bias vine to 5 of the creased 8" pale yellow blocks. Appliqué the pieces in this order to each background block: 1 length of vine, 1 or 2 A, 1 E, 1 F, and 1 G.

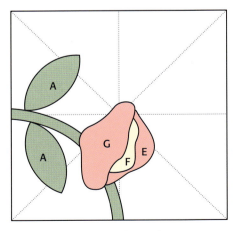

Setting square appliqué placement

5. Trace the templates and cut 3 A pieces from the assorted light green prints, 3 each of pieces B and D from the assorted light and medium pink fabrics, and 3 C pieces from the assorted yellow fabrics. Add a scant ¼" seam allowance to each fabric shape.

6. Position and pin the appliqués and the remaining strips of light green bias vine to the remaining 3 creased pale yellow blocks. Appliqué the pieces in this order to each background block: 1 length of vine, 1 A, 1 B, 1 C, and 1 D.

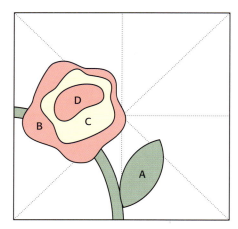

Setting square appliqué placement

7. Position and pin a length of dark green vine to 12 of the black side setting triangles as shown on page 33. Appliqué the vines in place.

8. Trace the templates and cut 12 A pieces from the assorted dark green prints, 4 each of pieces B and D from the assorted medium pink and burgundy fabrics, 4 C pieces from the assorted yellow and gold fabrics, 8 each of pieces E and G from assorted burgundy fabrics, and 8 F pieces from assorted yellow and gold fabrics. Add a scant ¼" seam allowance to each fabric shape. Set these pieces aside for now.

Assembly

1. Arrange the Nine Patch blocks, the 8" plain and appliquéd yellow setting squares, the plain and appliquéd side setting triangles, and the corner setting triangles as shown below. Be certain that you have placed the various appliquéd squares and triangles correctly.

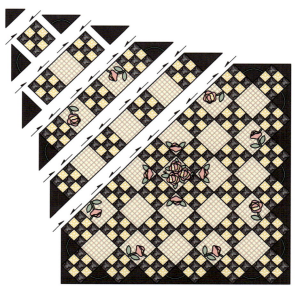

Assembly diagram

2. Pin, then sew, the blocks, squares, and side setting triangles to make 11 diagonal rows as shown. Press seams toward the pieced blocks.

3. With right sides together, and pinning carefully to match seams, sew the rows together. Press. Add corner setting triangles to complete the quilt center. The setting triangles are slightly oversized, so you'll need to square up the quilt before proceeding. Don't forget to leave a ¼"-wide seam allowance all around the outside edge!

¼" seam
allowance

4. With right sides together, and matching ends and midpoints, sew a black border strip to each side of the quilt top. Begin and end stitching ¼" from each corner of the quilt with a backstitch. The curved edges of the border will extend a few inches beyond the edges of the quilt top.

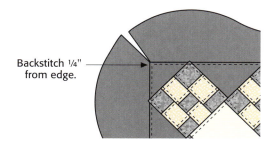

Backstitch ¼"
from edge.

5. Complete the corners by stitching the mitered corner with a ¼"-wide seam. Begin with a backstitch at the point where the long border seams end, and stitch toward the outer edge of each curved corner. Press long seams toward the border and the mitered seams to one side.

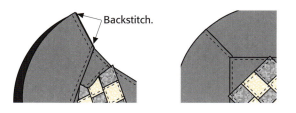

Backstitch.

6. Appliqué a remaining leaf and layered flower to each appliquéd setting triangle. Be sure flowers and leaves are positioned correctly to create a smoothly flowing vine. Notice that some of the appliqués overlap the border.

Setting triangle appliqué placement

Making and Appliquéing the Bees

Use the tan/black stripe and light tan scraps to make 16 bees. Appliqué the bees randomly across the quilt, using the photo on page 28 for guidance.

Layering and Finishing

1. Divide the backing fabric crosswise into 2 panels of approximately 85" each. Remove the selvages and join the pieces to make a single, large backing panel.

2. Center and layer the quilt top and batting over the backing; baste.

3. Quilt as desired. Trim the backing and batting to match the quilt top.

4. Use the binding fabric to cut a total of 375" of 2¾"-wide bias binding strips. Sew the binding to the quilt. The bias will handle the gentle curves smoothly.

5. Make a label and attach it to your quilt.

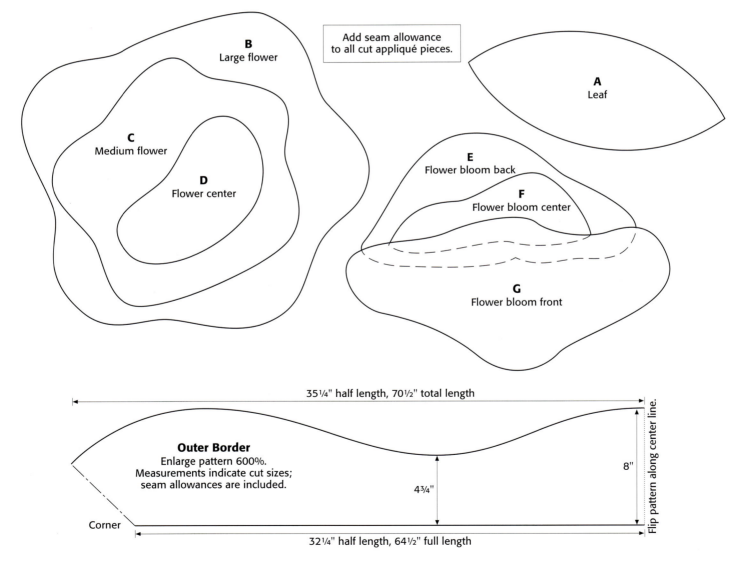

B
Large flower

Add seam allowance to all cut appliqué pieces.

A
Leaf

C
Medium flower

D
Flower center

E
Flower bloom back

F
Flower bloom center

G
Flower bloom front

35¼" half length, 70½" total length

Outer Border
Enlarge pattern 600%.
Measurements indicate cut sizes; seam allowances are included.

4¾"

8"

Flip pattern along center line.

Corner

32¼" half length, 64½" full length

Butterflight

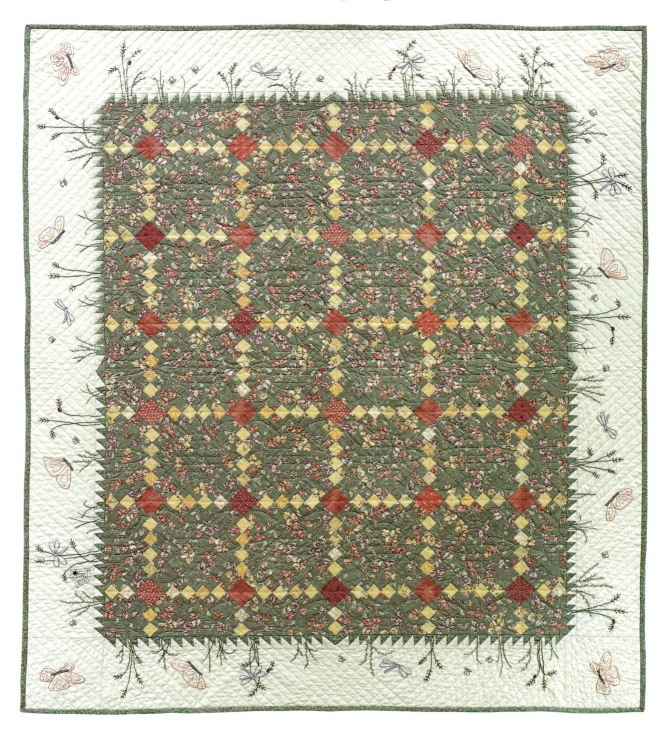

BUTTERFLIGHT by Linda Johnson, 1999, Auburn, Washington, 57" x 65½".

A NOTE ABOUT BUTTERFLIES

THE BUTTERFLY IS the classic harbinger of spring and nature's rebirth. No one (other than kids!) really likes caterpillars, but as soon as they become butterflies, they're magic, spreading hope wherever they flit.

FINISHED QUILT SIZE: 57" x 65½"
FINISHED BLOCK SIZE: 6"

Materials

42"-wide fabric

- ½ yd. *total* of assorted yellow prints for blocks
- 2⅛ yds. green print fabric for blocks, setting squares, and setting triangles
- ¼ yd. *total* of assorted pink prints for blocks
- 1⅝ yds. muslin for sawtooth and outer borders
- 1 yd. green solid or subtle print for sawtooth border and bias binding
- 3½ yds. fabric for backing
- 60" x 69" piece of batting
- Erasable marker
- No. 8 perle cotton thread in 2 different pinks or peaches, and yellow*
- No. 5 perle cotton thread in 2 different greens*
- 1 skein *each* of black, gray, and red embroidery floss*

* These are basic colors required for the embroidery in this quilt. You may add other colors if you wish.

Cutting

All cutting measurements include ¼"-wide seam allowances.

From the assorted yellow prints, cut a *total* of:
- 9 strips, 1½" x 42", for blocks

From the green print fabric cut:
- 9 strips, each 1½" x 42", for blocks
- 8 strips, each 2½" x 42", for blocks. Crosscut strips into 120 squares, each 2½" x 2½".
- 4 strips, each 6½" x 42", for setting squares. Crosscut strips into 20 squares, each 6½" x 6½".
- 5 squares, each 9¾" x 9¾", for side setting triangles. Cut squares twice diagonally to make 20 triangles.
- 2 squares, each 5" x 5", for corner setting triangles. Cut squares once diagonally to make 4 triangles.

From the assorted pink print fabrics, cut:
- 30 squares, each 2½" x 2½", for blocks

From the muslin, cut:
- 2 strips, each 6½" x 43", from *length* of fabric for outer border

- 2 strips, each 6½" x 51½", from *length* of fabric for outer border
- 3 strips each 3⅞" x 42", for sawtooth border. Crosscut strips into 22 squares, each 3⅞" x 3⅞".
- 4 squares, each 7½" x 7½", for outer border corner squares

From the green solid or subtle print, cut:

- 3 strips, each 3⅞" x 42", for sawtooth border. Crosscut strips into 22 squares, each 3⅞" x 3⅞".

Note: *Refer to "General Instructions" (pages 6–18) as needed for guidance with all basic construction techniques.*

Making the Blocks

You'll need 30 pieced blocks for this quilt.

1. Pair each 1½" x 42" yellow print strip with a 1½" x 42" green print strip. With right sides together, sew along one long raw edge to make a total of 9 strip sets. Press seams toward the green strip. Each strip set should measure 2½" x 42" when sewn and pressed.

2. Crosscut strip sets into 1½" segments. Cut a *total* of 240 segments.

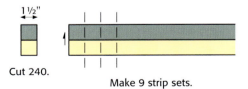

Cut 240.

Make 9 strip sets.

3. Stitch segments from step 2 in pairs to make a total of 120 four-patch units. Press.

Make 120.

4. Sew one 2½" green print square between 2 four-patch units from step 3, positioning four-patch units carefully as shown. Press seams toward green square. Make 60.

5. Sew each 2½" pink print square between 2 remaining 2½" green print squares. Make 30. Press seams toward green squares.

6. Sew each unit from step 5 between 2 units from step 4. Press.

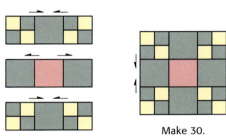

Make 30.

Assembly

1. Refer to the assembly diagram below and the photo on page 35. Arrange the blocks, the 6½" green setting squares, the side setting triangles, and the corner setting triangles as shown.

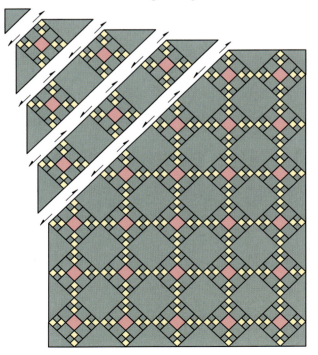

Assembly diagram

2. Pin, and then sew the blocks, squares, and side setting triangles to make 10 diagonal rows. Press seams toward the setting squares.

3. With right sides together, and pinning carefully to match seams, sew the rows together. Press. Add corner setting triangles to complete the quilt center. Square up the quilt top as necessary, making sure to leave a ¼"-wide seam allowance all around the outside edge! (See "Assembly" step 3 on page 32.)

Making the Sawtooth Border

1. Use a pencil to draw a vertical and horizontal line on the back of each 3⅞" muslin square, dividing the square into quarters. Draw a second set of lines, this time dividing the block diagonally in both directions.

2. With right sides together, pair each 3⅞" marked muslin square with a 3⅞" green solid or subtle print square. Stitch ¼" from both sides of each diagonal line.

3. Use your rotary cutter and ruler to cut along all pencil-marked vertical, horizontal, and diagonal lines. Unfold half-square triangle units and press seams toward the green triangles. You'll have 176 half-square triangle units, each measuring 1½" square.

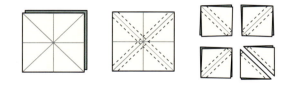

4. Arrange 20 half-square triangle units from step 3 to make a horizontal row as shown. Sew units together and press seams to one side. Make 2 rows. Repeat to make 2 additional 20-unit rows, this time reversing the direction of the triangles as shown.

Make 2 of each.

5. Arrange 24 remaining half-square triangle units to make a horizontal row as shown. Sew units together and press to one side. Make 2 rows. Repeat, reversing the direction of the triangles to make 2 additional 24-unit rows.

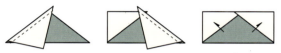

Make 2 of each.

6. Use the patterns on page 40 to make templates for pieces A–D. From scraps of muslin, cut 2 each of pieces A, A reverse, C, and C reverse. From scraps of green solid or subtle print, cut 2 each of pieces B and D.

7. Sew an A piece to one short side of each B piece. Press toward the B triangles. Repeat to sew an A reverse piece to the other short side of the B piece. Press. Make 2.

8. Repeat step 7, this time sewing a C and C reverse piece to opposite short sides of each D piece. Press toward the C triangles.

Make 2.
Finished size: 2½" x 1"

Make 2.
Finished size: 3" x 1"

To keep instructions as simple as possible, templates are given for the A/B and C/D sawtooth border units. If you prefer, you may use the foundation piecing method to construct these units, as I did. To draft paper foundation patterns, add ¼" seam allowances to the following dimensions: The finished size of the A/B unit is 2 ½" x 1". The finished size of the C/D unit is 3" x 1". You will need 2 of each unit.

Making the Embroidered Borders

1. Referring to the embroidery patterns on pages 41–45 and the photo on page 35 as a guide, use an erasable marker to trace embroidery motifs onto the 4 muslin border strips. Modify the arrangement and number of motifs as you wish. Use the entire motif in some places and just part of the motif in others.

2. Use the No. 5 perle cotton thread to embroider the grass, and various colors of No. 8 perle cotton thread and embroidery floss to embroider the butterflies, dragonflies, ladybugs, spiderweb and bees.

3. Use the pattern on page 40 to trace the corner butterfly motif onto each of the 7½" muslin squares. Use the various colors of perle cotton thread and embroidery floss to embroider the motifs.

9. Sew each unit from step 7 between 1 regular and 1 reverse 20-unit row from step 4. Press. Make 2 identical rows.

10. Sew each pieced row from step 9 to one 6½" x 43" muslin outer border strip and press. Refer to the photo on page 35 for guidance in positioning the sawtooth strip.

11. Sew each unit from step 8 between 1 regular and 1 reverse 24-unit row from step 5. Press. Make 2 identical rows.

12. Sew each pieced row from step 11 to one 6½" x 51½" muslin outer border strip and press.

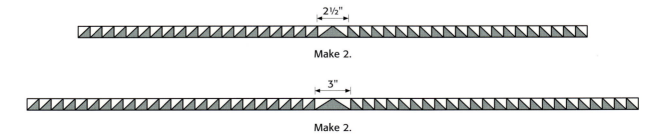

2½"

Make 2.

3"

Make 2.

4. With right sides together, and matching ends and midpoints, sew the 51½" embroidered borders to the long sides of the quilt top. Be sure the sawtooth row is positioned next to the quilt center. Press seams toward the quilt center.

5. Sew a 7½" embroidered corner square to both short ends of each 43" embroidered border strip. Refer to the photo on page 35 to be certain you are positioning the butterflies properly.

6. Repeat step 4 to sew the 43" border strips to the top and bottom edges of the quilt. Press.

Layering and Finishing

1. Divide the backing fabric crosswise into 2 equal panels of approximately 63" each. Remove the selvages and join the pieces to make a single, large backing panel.

2. Center and layer the quilt top and batting over the backing. The backing seam should run parallel to the top and bottom edges of the quilt top. Baste.

3. Quilt as desired.

4. Use the remaining green solid or subtle print fabric to cut a total of 260" of 2¾"-wide bias binding strips. Sew the binding to the quilt.

5. Make and attach a label to the quilt.

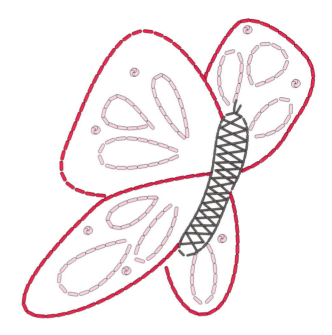

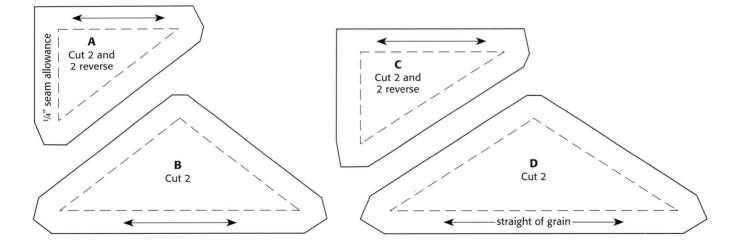

¼" seam allowance

A
Cut 2 and
2 reverse

B
Cut 2

C
Cut 2 and
2 reverse

D
Cut 2

straight of grain

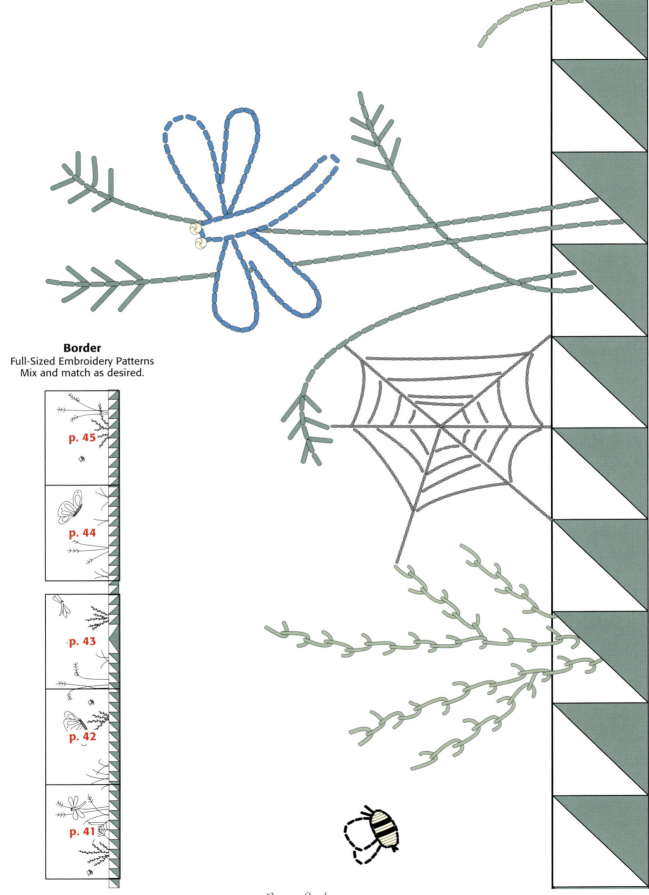

Border
Full-Sized Embroidery Patterns
Mix and match as desired.

p. 45

p. 44

p. 43

p. 42

p. 41

Connect to pattern on page 41.

Pattern continues on page 44.

Connect to pattern on page 42.

Connect to pattern on page 45.

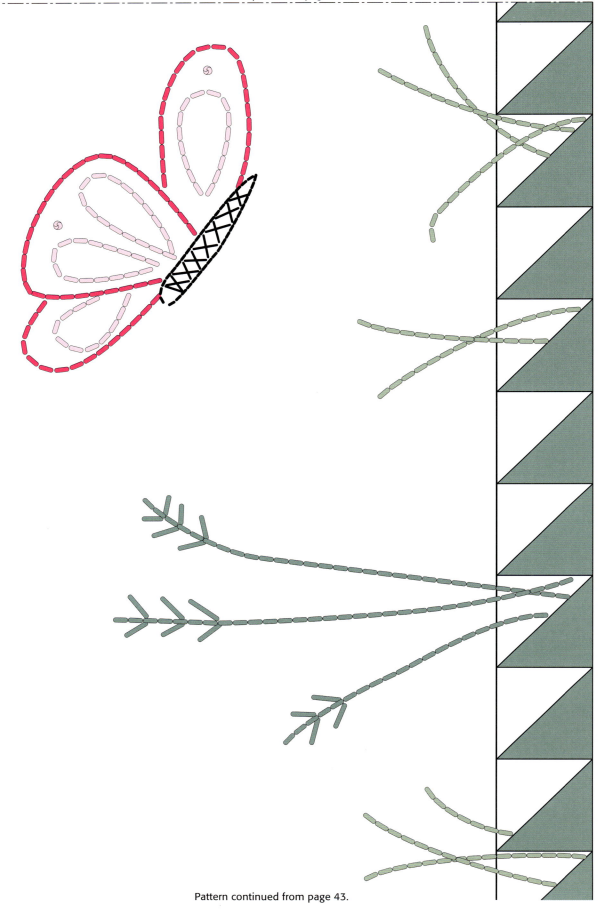

Pattern continued from page 43.

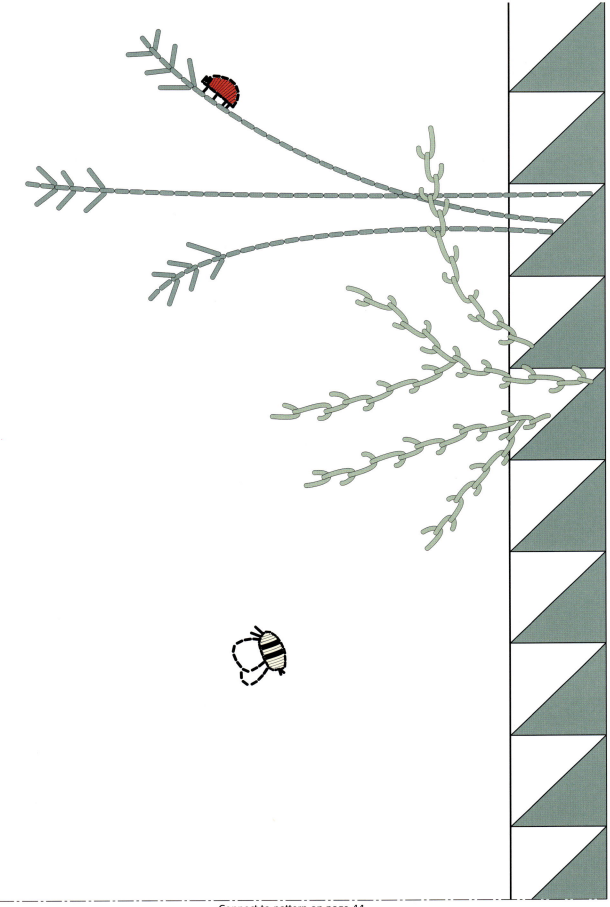

Connect to pattern on page 44.

Baby Blooms

BABY BLOOMS by Linda Johnson, 1999, Auburn, Washington, 43¾" x 43¾".

This simple quilt—with its single Irish Chain block and "fried-egg" flowers—cries out for pieces from your scrap bag. There are no bees here, because I wouldn't want the baby to be stung.

FINISHED QUILT SIZE: 43¾" x 43¾"
FINISHED BLOCK SIZE: 6¼" x 6¼"

Materials

42"-wide fabric

- ⅔ yd. *total* of assorted periwinkle and aqua prints for Irish Chain blocks
- 1⅝ yds. muslin for Irish Chain and muslin blocks
- 8 squares, each 6" x 6", of assorted peach and pink prints for flower appliqués
- Assorted yellow scraps for flower appliqués
- ¼ yd. *total* of assorted light green scraps for leaf appliqués
- ⅝ yd. periwinkle print for bias binding
- 2¾ yds. fabric for backing
- 47" x 47" piece of batting

Cutting

All cutting measurements include ¼"-wide seam allowances.

From the periwinkle and aqua prints, cut a total of:

- 225 squares, each 1¾" x 1¾", for Irish Chain blocks

From the muslin, cut:

- 4 strips, each 6¾" x 42". Crosscut strips into 24 squares, each 6¾" x 6¾", for muslin blocks.
- 16 strips, each 1¾" x 42". Crosscut strips into 100 rectangles, each 1¾" x 4¼", and 100 squares, each 1¾" x 1¾", for Irish Chain blocks.

Note: *Refer to "General Instructions" (pages 6–18) as needed for guidance and all basic construction techniques.*

Making the Blocks

You'll need 25 Irish Chain blocks for this quilt.

1. Arrange five 1¾" periwinkle and/or aqua squares and four 1¾" muslin squares in 3 rows as shown. Sew the squares into rows. Press seams away from the muslin squares.

2. Pinning carefully to match seams, sew the rows together to make a nine-patch unit. Press seams in one direction.

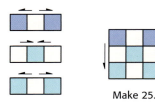

Make 25.

3. Sew a 1¾" x 4¼" muslin rectangle to opposite sides of the nine-patch unit. Press seams away from the rectangles.

4. Sew a 1¾" periwinkle or aqua square to the short ends of a 1¾" x 4½" muslin rectangle. Press seams toward the squares.

5. Sew the unit from step 3 between the 2 units from step 4 and press.

6. Repeat steps 1–5 to make a total of 25 blocks.

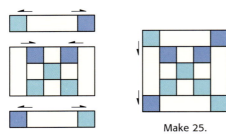

Make 25.

Assembly

1. Refer to the assembly diagram below and the photo on page 46. Arrange alternating 6¾" Irish Chain and muslin blocks in 7 horizontal rows of 7 blocks each. Odd-numbered rows begin with pieced blocks, while even-numbered rows begin with plain blocks.

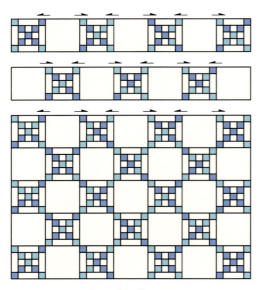

Assembly diagram

2. Pin and sew the blocks into rows. Press seams toward the pieced blocks.

3. With right sides together, and pinning carefully to match seams, sew the rows together. Press seams in one direction.

Appliquéing the "Fried-Egg" Flowers

1. Use the patterns on page 49 to make templates for pattern pieces A–C. Trace the templates and cut 8 A pieces from the 6" squares of assorted pink and peach prints, 8 B pieces from the assorted yellow scraps, and 24 C pieces from the assorted light green fabrics. Add a scant ¼" seam allowance to each fabric shape.

2. Refer to the photo on page 46. Scatter and pin 8 "fried-egg" flowers over the surface of the quilt. Each flower includes 1 each of pieces A and B, and 3 C pieces.

3. Appliqué the pieces in alphabetical order to the quilt top.

Layering and Finishing

1. Divide the backing fabric crosswise into 2 equal pieces of approximately 49" each. Remove the selvages and join the pieces to make a single, large backing panel.

2. Center and layer the quilt top and batting over the backing; baste.

3. Quilt as desired.

4. Use the periwinkle print fabric to cut a total of 190" of 2¾"-wide bias binding strips. Sew the binding to the quilt.

5. Make a label and attach it to your quilt.

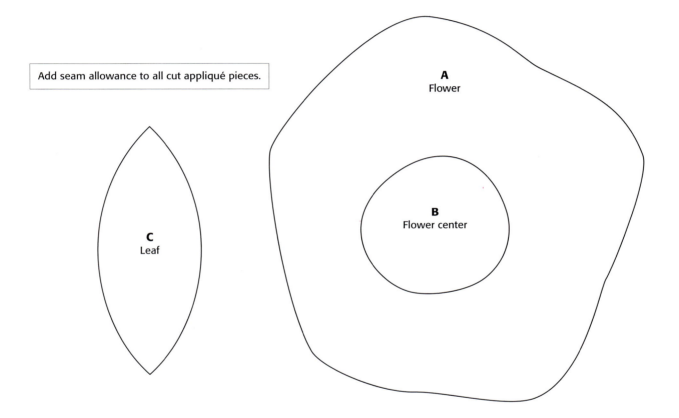

Add seam allowance to all cut appliqué pieces.

A
Flower

B
Flower center

C
Leaf

For You

FOR YOU by Linda Johnson, 1999, Auburn, Washington, 26¾" x 36¾".

*I*magine that you are in the kitchen, up to your elbows in dirty dishes, when the back door bursts open. Your grubby three-year-old bundle of energy runs in to hand you a bouquet of wilted dandelions, then runs back out. You look at them, and this is what you see...

FINISHED QUILT SIZE: 26¾" x 36¾"

Materials

42"-wide fabric

- ⅜ yd. *total* of assorted lavender prints for Nine Patch blocks, corner squares, and flower appliqués
- 1 yd. muslin for Nine Patch blocks, sashing, and appliqué background
- Assorted yellow print scraps for flower and ribbon appliqués
- ⅓ yd. *total* of assorted light green prints for leaf and stem appliqués
- Tan/black stripe scrap for bee appliqué
- Light tan scrap for bee wing appliqués
- ½ yd. lavender print for bias binding
- ⅞ yd. fabric for backing
- 32" x 42" piece of batting
- Erasable marker
- 1 skein medium purple embroidery floss
- Architect's plastic ellipse template

Cutting

All cutting measurements include ¼"-wide seam allowances.

From the assorted lavender prints, cut a *total* of:
- 140 squares, each 1¾" x 1¾", for Nine Patch blocks and corner squares

From the muslin, cut:
- 1 piece, 14¼" x 24¼", for appliqué background
- 10 strips, each 1¾" x 42". Crosscut strips into 60 rectangles, each 1¾" x 4¼", for sashing, and 80 squares, each 1¾" x 1¾", for Nine Patch blocks.

Note: *Refer to "General Instructions" (pages 6–18) as needed for guidance with all basic construction techniques.*

Making the Pieced Blocks

You'll need 20 Nine Patch blocks for this quilt. The blocks are joined with sashing and corner squares.

1. Arrange five 1¾" lavender print squares and four 1¾" muslin squares in 3 rows as shown. Sew the squares into rows. Press seams toward the lavender squares.

2. Pin carefully to match seams, and sew the rows together to make a block. Press seams in one direction. Make 20.

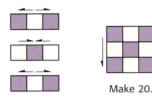

Make 20.

3. Sew a 1¾" x 4¼" muslin sashing rectangle to opposite sides of each Nine Patch block. Press seams away from the rectangles. Label these units Block A.

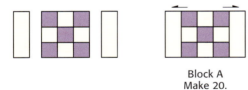

Block A
Make 20.

4. Sew a remaining 1¾" lavender square to the short ends of each remaining 1¾" x 4¼" muslin rectangle. Press seams toward the squares.

5. Sew a Block A unit between 2 units from step 4. Press seams toward the center unit. Make 10. Label these units Block B.

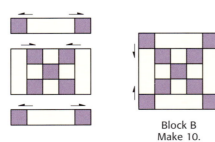

Block B
Make 10.

Assembly

1. Arrange 3 of Block B and 2 of Block A in a row, alternating them as shown. Pin and sew the blocks and press seams as desired. Make 2 rows.

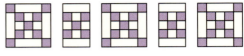

Make 2 rows.

2. Arrange 3 of Block A and 2 of Block B in a row, alternating them as shown. Pin and sew the blocks and press seams as desired. Make 2 rows.

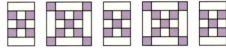

Make 2 rows.

3. Fold the 14¼" x 24¼" muslin background piece in quarters to find its center. These fold lines will assist you later in placing the appliqué design on the background fabric.

4. With right sides together, and ends and midpoints matched, sew a row from step 2 to each long side of the 14¼" x 24¼" muslin piece. Press seams away from the center panel.

5. Sew a row from step 1 to the top and bottom of the quilt. Press.

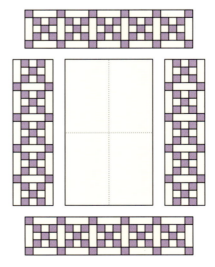

Appliquéing the Center Panel

1. Use the patterns on page 55 to make templates for pieces A–E. Trace the templates and cut 4 A pieces from the assorted lavender prints, 4 each of pieces B and C from the assorted yellow and lavender prints, 7 D pieces from the assorted green prints, and 1 E piece from the assorted yellow prints. Add a scant ¼" seam allowance to each fabric shape. Refer to the photo on page 50 for guidance as needed.

2. Cut a total of 3 bias strips, each ⅞" x 16", from the assorted light green prints.

3. Referring to the appliqué placement diagram below, lay out and pin the 3 bias stems and appliqué pieces A, B, and C on the muslin background piece. Position and pin the 7 leaves (piece D), tucking 4 of them behind the flowers as greenery. Pin piece E over the 3 stems at the place where they touch, as shown.

Appliqué placement

4. Appliqué the pieces in this order to the background block: stems, leaves (D), A, B, C, and E. Be sure the bottom end of each stem is cut and stitched at an angle as shown. Trim leaves under flowers to reduce bulk.

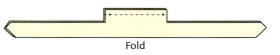

5. Use the pattern on page 55 to make a template for the "3-dimensional" ribbon (F). Trace the template to cut one bow piece from the remaining yellow print scraps.

6. Fold the ribbon in half lengthwise right sides together, matching the dots. Sew from raw edge to raw edge, taking a ¼"-wide seam. Finger press the seam open.

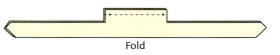

Fold

7. Turn the ribbon right side out. Press, centering the stitched seam and turning under a ¼"-wide seam allowance along the long raw edges.

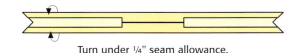

Turn under ¼" seam allowance.

8. Tie the ribbon in a single knot. Position the knot over piece E on the appliquéd bouquet, seamed side down, and pin. Arrange the ribbon tails, trim them as desired, and appliqué the entire ribbon in place for a 3-D effect.

9. Use the tan/black stripe and light tan scraps to make 1 bee. Appliqué the bee in place as shown in the appliqué placement diagram.

10. Refer to the appliqué placement diagram and the photo on page 50. Use the pattern below and an erasable marker to trace the words *for you* onto the appliquéd panel.

11. Use the medium purple embroidery floss and a backstitch to embroider the words onto the muslin.

Layering and Finishing

1. Center and layer the quilt top and batting over the backing; baste.

2. Quilt as desired.

3. Use the ½ yard of lavender print fabric to cut a total of 142" of 2¾"-wide bias binding strips. Sew the binding to the quilt.

4. Make a label and attach it to your quilt.

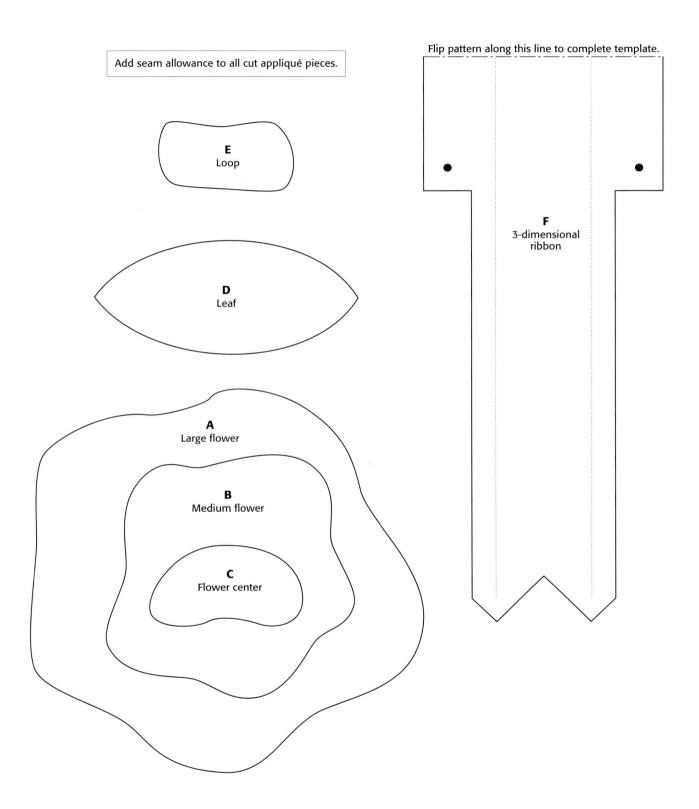

Add seam allowance to all cut appliqué pieces.

E
Loop

Flip pattern along this line to complete template.

F
3-dimensional
ribbon

D
Leaf

A
Large flower

B
Medium flower

C
Flower center

Are You My Mother?

<small>ARE YOU MY MOTHER? by Linda Johnson, 1999, Auburn, Washington, 21" x 27½".</small>

Remember the children's story by P. D. Eastman? A little bird is seeking his mother, asking anyone he meets, "Are you my mother?"

FINISHED QUILT SIZE: 21" x 27½"

Materials

42"-wide fabric

- ¾ yd. muslin for appliqué background and outer border
- Assorted dark pink, light pink, and yellow scraps for hollyhock appliqués
- Assorted green scraps for hollyhock appliqués and stem and leaf appliqués
- Assorted gray and moss green scraps for rock appliqués
- Assorted blue scraps for bird and dragonfly appliqués
- ½ yd. periwinkle print for inner border and bias binding
- ⅞ yd. fabric for backing
- 24" x 32" piece of batting
- Erasable marker
- Black, dark pink, light pink, and yellow embroidery floss

Cutting

All cutting measurements include ¼"-wide seam allowances.

From the muslin, cut:
- 1 piece, 15½" x 22½", for appliqué background
- 2 strips, each 3" x 23½", for outer border
- 2 strips, each 3" x 21½", for outer border

From the assorted green scraps, cut:
- 1 strip, 1" x 19½", for stems*
- 1 strip, 1" x 17½", for stems*
- 1 strip, 1" x 14½", for stems*

From the periwinkle print, cut:
- 2 strips, each 1" x 22½", for inner border
- 2 strips, each 1" x 16½", for inner border

* Since the stems in this quilt are straight rather than curved, strips may be cut on the straight grain.

Note: *Refer to "General Instructions" (pages 6–18) as needed for guidance with all basic construction techniques.*

Preparing the Center Panel for Appliqué

1. Fold the 15½" x 22½" muslin background piece in quarters to find its center. These fold lines will assist you in placing the appliqué design on the background fabric.

2. Use the patterns on page 60 to make templates for pieces A–O. Trace the templates and cut a total of 2 A pieces, 7 B pieces, 8 C pieces, and 1 D piece from the assorted pink and yellow scraps; 9 E pieces, 1 F and 1 F reverse piece, 3 G and 1 G reverse pieces, 6 H and 2 H reverse pieces, and 1 I piece from the assorted green scraps; 1 each of pieces J, K, and L from the gray and moss green scraps; 1 M piece from the yellow scraps; and 1 each of pieces N and O from the assorted blue scraps. Add a scant ¼" seam allowance to each fabric shape.

3. Use a ruler and an erasable marker to mark 3 vertical lines on the 15½" x 22½" muslin piece as shown. Begin each line at the bottom edge of the block. Beginning from the left, the marked lines should measure 19½", 14½", and 17½" high. These will serve as guidelines for placing the stems.

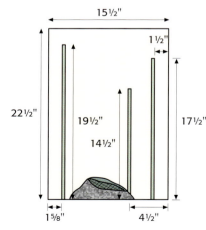

4. Position each stem over the line of matching length that you have marked on the background panel. Appliqué the stems in place. Do not turn under the short raw edges.

5. Referring to the appliqué placement diagram on page 59 and the photo on page 56, position and pin pieces J, K, and L to the muslin background. The raw edge of piece K should be even with the bottom raw edge of the muslin panel. Appliqué the pieces in alphabetical order to the background.

6. Sew the 1" x 22½" inner border strips to the sides of the muslin background panel, and the 1" x 16½" inner border strips to the top and bottom. Press. The lower edge of piece K and the bottom ends of the stems will be sewn into the seam.

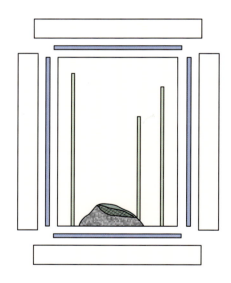

7. Repeat step 6 to sew the 3" x 23½" outer border strips to the sides and the 3" x 21½" outer border strips to the top and bottom of the quilt. Press.

Completing the Appliqué and Embroidery

1. Referring to the appliqué placement diagram at right and the photo on page 56, lay out and pin pieces A–I, M, N, and O to the partially appliquéd center panel. Notice that the 2 largest leaves (F and F reverse) overlap the bottom borders.

2. Appliqué pieces A–I to the background, beginning with the pieces that will be overlapped by other appliqués. Finish by appliquéing M, N, and O, in that order.

3. Use blue scraps to make and appliqué 1 dragonfly. Refer to the appliqué placement diagram as needed.

4. Use yellow embroidery floss to make French-knot eyes for the dragonfly and black embroidery floss to backstitch the dragonfly's legs and the bird's feet. Use the black floss to make a French-knot eye for the bird. Using floss that coordinates with the flowers, embroider a "star" on some of the E appliqués. They will appear to be buds just starting to open.

Layering and Finishing

1. Center and layer the quilt top and batting over the backing; baste.

2. Quilt as desired.

3. Use the remaining periwinkle print fabric to cut a total of 112" of 2¾"-wide bias binding strips. Sew the binding to the quilt.

4. Make a label and attach it to your quilt.

Appliqué placement diagram

Add seam allowance to all cut appliqué pieces.

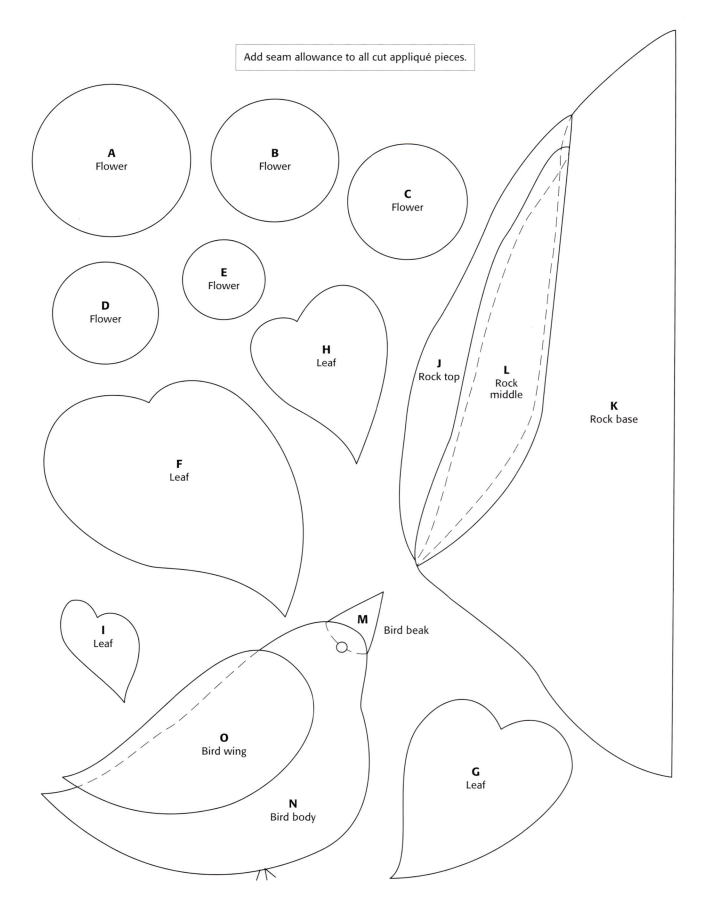

Aphid Harvest

APHID HARVEST by Linda Johnson, 1999, Auburn, Washington, 22½" x 22½".

*N*o, these are not Greek olives with pimentos growing on vines! They are wonderful, hungry ladybugs. Ladybugs are among my favorite bugs because they eat aphids—one of my least favorite bugs. Every year we host the Winter Ladybug Festival in our upstairs bedrooms. All we need is one sunny day and voilà: there they are!

A NOTE ABOUT LADYBUGS

LADYBUGS, ALSO KNOWN as ladybird beetles, are voracious eaters. They can consume twenty to thirty aphids a day as larvae, and even more as adults. We have a huge tulip tree next to our house that gets covered with aphids each summer. I love to see the ladybugs arrive!

FINISHED QUILT SIZE: 22½" x 22½"
FINISHED BLOCK SIZE: 4"

Materials

42"-wide fabric

- ⅜ yd. muslin for Four Patch blocks and setting squares
- ⅛ yd. *total* of assorted '30s reproduction prints
- ⅓ yd. yellow print for inner border and bias binding
- ¼ yd. red print for outer border
- ¼ yd. *total* of assorted green print scraps for leaves
- ⅛ yd. red tone-on-tone print for ladybugs
- ¾ yd. fabric for backing

- 25" x 25" piece of batting
- Erasable marker
- No. 5 green perle cotton thread
- Architect's plastic circle template
- Black Pigma pen

Cutting

All cutting measurements include ¼"-wide seam allowances.

From the muslin, cut:

- 1 strip, 4½" x 42". Crosscut strip into 8 squares, each 4½" x 4½", for setting squares.
- 1 strip, 2½" x 42". Crosscut strip into 16 squares, each 2½" x 2½", for Four Patch blocks.

From the assorted reproduction prints, cut a *total* of:

- 16 squares, each 2½" x 2½", for Four Patch blocks

From the yellow print, cut:

- 2 strips, each 1" x 16½", for inner border
- 2 strips, each 1" x 17½", for inner border

From the red print, cut:

- 2 strips, each 3" x 17½", for outer border
- 2 strips, each 3" x 22½", for outer border

> **Note:** *Refer to "General Instructions" (pages 6–18) as needed for guidance with all basic construction techniques.*

Making the Blocks

You'll need 8 Four Patch blocks for this quilt.

1. Arrange two 2½" muslin squares and two 2½" print squares in 2 rows as shown. Sew the squares into rows. Press seams toward print squares.

2. Pin carefully to match seams, and sew the rows together to make a block. Press seams in one direction. Make 8.

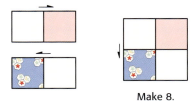

Make 8.

Assembly

1. Arrange alternating 4½" Four Patch and muslin blocks in 4 horizontal rows of 4 blocks each. Odd-numbered rows begin with pieced blocks,

while even-numbered rows begin with muslin blocks.

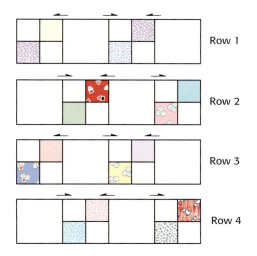

Row 1

Row 2

Row 3

Row 4

2. Pin and sew the block into rows. Press seams toward the pieced blocks.

3. With right sides together, and pinning carefully to match seams, sew the rows together. Press seams in one direction.

4. Sew the 1" x 16½" inner border strips to the sides of the quilt and the 1" x 17½" inner border strips to the top and bottom. Press seams toward the border strips.

5. Sew the 3" x 17½" outer border strips to the sides, and the 3" x 22½" outer border strips to the top and bottom of the quilt. Press.

Adding the Appliqué and Embroidery

1. Use the pattern on page 64 and an erasable marker to trace the vine onto the quilt top, placing tendrils as desired.

2. Use the No. 5 green perle cotton thread and a backstitch to embroider the vines on the quilt.

Make 2 rows of stitching, staggering the stitches so there are no gaps. Use a single row of stitching for the tendrils.

3. Use the pattern below to make a template for the leaf. Trace the template and cut 32 leaves from the assorted green scraps. Add a scant ¼" seam allowance to each fabric shape.

4. Referring to the project diagram and the photo of the quilt, pin the leaves to the quilt. Notice that some of the leaves overlap the inner borders. Appliqué the leaves to the quilt.

5. Refer to "Ladybugs" on page 12. Use the architect's template, the red tone-on-tone scraps, and a black Pigma pen to make 14 ladybug appliqués. Appliqué the ladybugs to the quilt, referring to the project diagram as needed.

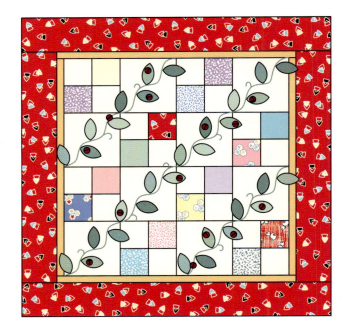

Layering and Finishing

1. Center and layer the quilt top and batting over the backing; baste.

2. Quilt as desired.

3. Use the remaining yellow fabric to cut a total of 112" of 2¾"-wide bias binding. Sew the binding to the quilt.

4. Make a label and attach it to your quilt.

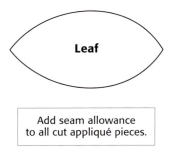

Leaf

Add seam allowance to all cut appliqué pieces.

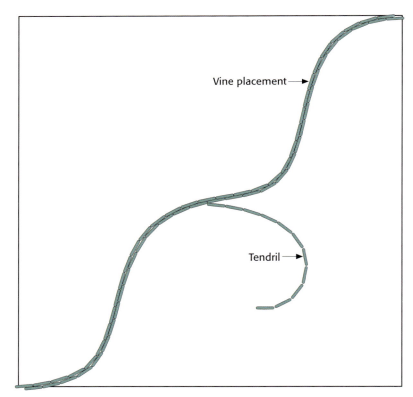

Vine placement →

Tendril →

Embroidery pattern for 1 block
Alter tendril placement as desired.

Dragonfly Pillow

DRAGONFLY PILLOW by Linda Johnson, 1999, Auburn, Washington, 11½" x 11½".

A NOTE ABOUT DRAGONFLIES

The dragonfly is a gentle insect. It is distinguished from its cousin the damselfly by the way it holds its wings at rest. The dragonfly holds its wings horizontally at its sides and the damselfly holds its wings vertically over its back. They are both wonderful creatures because they eat mosquitoes. Anyone rooting for the mosquitoes?

FINISHED SIZE: 11½" x 11½"

Materials

42"-wide fabric

- One 6" x 6" muslin square for background
- Assorted blue and purple scraps for log cabin–style border
- One 12" x 12" square of fabric for backing
- Erasable marker
- One 6" x 6" square of freezer paper
- 1 skein each of blue and purple embroidery floss
- Brown Pigma pen
- 1 package of stuffing

Cutting

All cutting measurements include ¼"-wide seam allowances.

From the assorted blue and purple scraps, cut a *total* of:
- 1 strip, 1½" x 6"
- 1 strip, 1½" x 7"
- 1 strip, 2½" x 7"
- 1 strip, 1½" x 9"
- 1 strip, 2½" x 8"
- 1 strip, 2½" x 11"
- 1 strip, 1½" x 10"
- 1 strip, 2½" x 12"

(all for log cabin–style border)

Note: *Refer to "General Instructions" (pages 6–18) as needed for guidance with all basic construction techniques.*

Assembly

1. Fold the 6" muslin square in quarters to find its center, then crease the block on both diagonals. These fold lines will assist you in centering the embroidery design on the background block.

2. Use the full-size pattern on page 68 and an erasable marker to trace the dragonfly motif onto the muslin square.

3. Use 2 strands of blue embroidery floss and a backstitch to embroider the outline of the dragonfly on the muslin square. Use the blue embroidery floss to make French-knot eyes.

4. Use a single strand of blue embroidery floss to work straight stitches on each section of the body. Add texture to the dragonfly wings by using a single strand of blue embroidery floss to work straight stitches in a random vertical pattern. Use a single strand of purple floss to work straight stitches in a random horizontal pattern on the wings.

5. Remove any markings that may be set by heat, and then iron the 6" square of freezer paper shiny side down to the back of the embroidered muslin square. Use the pattern on page 68 and a brown Pigma pen to trace the words *dragonfly* and *Plathemis lybia* onto the muslin. The freezer paper will help stabilize the block as you write. Remove the freezer paper.

6. Refer to the assembly diagram below. Sew the 1½" x 6" strip to the top edge of the embroidered block. Press seams toward the strip. Continue adding strips in alphabetical order to the embroidered block, working in a clockwise direction. Press each strip as it is added.

7. Place the completed pillow top and the 12" square of backing fabric right sides together with raw edges aligned.. Stitch a ¼" seam all around the outside edge, leaving a 5" opening along one side.

8. Turn the pillow right side out and stuff.

9. Hand stitch the opening closed.

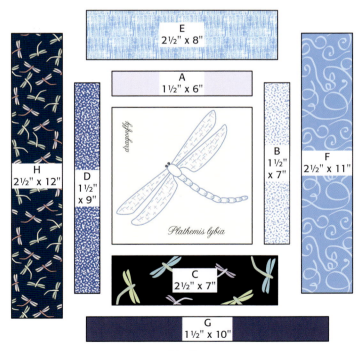

Assembly diagram
Measurements shown are *cut* sizes.

dragonfly

Plathemis lybia

Potted Posy Pillow

POTTED POSY PILLOW by Linda Johnson, 1999, Auburn, Washington, 16¼" x 16¼".

FINISHED SIZE: 16¼" x 16¼"

Materials

42"-wide fabric

- ½ yd. muslin for checkerboard border and appliqué background
- ¼ yd. total of assorted '30s reproduction prints for checkerboard border
- Assorted red, pink, and yellow scraps for flower appliqués
- Assorted green scraps for leaves and stems
- One 6" x 6" square brown print for flowerpot appliqué
- Tan/black stripe scrap for bee appliqué
- Light tan scrap for bee wing appliqués
- ½ yd. fabric for backing
- 17" x 17" piece of batting
- Architect's plastic ellipse template
- Erasable marker
- 2 pieces of lightweight interfacing, each 2" x 16¾"
- 3 buttons, each 1" diameter
- 16" pillow form

Cutting

All cutting measurements include ¼"-wide seam allowances.

From the muslin, cut:

- 3 strips, each 1¾" x 42". Crosscut strips into 60 squares, each 1¾" x 1¾", for checkerboard border.
- 1 square, 9¼" x 9¼", for appliqué background

From the assorted reproduction prints, cut a *total* of:

- 60 squares, each 1¾" x 1¾", for checkerboard border

From the backing fabric, cut:

- 2 pieces, each 16¾" x 10⅞", for pillow back

    Note: *Refer to "General Instructions" (pages 6–18) as needed for guidance with all basic construction techniques.*

Assembling the Pillow Top

1. Referring to the diagram below, arrange alternating 1¾" muslin squares and 1¾" reproduction print squares in 3 rows of 13 squares each. Rows 1 and 3 begin with muslin squares, while row 2 begins with a print square.

2. Pin and sew the squares together into rows. Press seams toward the print squares.

3. With right sides together, and pinning carefully to match seams, sew the rows together. Press seams in one direction. Make 2 identical 3-row border units.

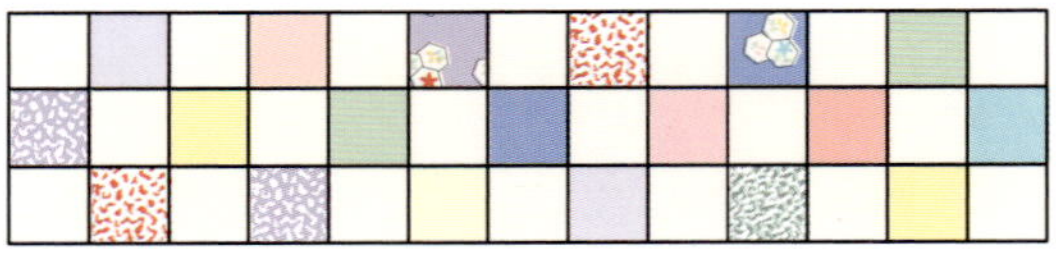

Make 2.

4. Arrange the remaining 1¾" muslin and 1¾" reproduction print squares into 3 rows of 7 squares each as shown on page 71. Rows 1 and 3 begin with print squares, while row 2 begins with a muslin square.

5. Repeat steps 2 and 3 to sew the blocks together into rows and the rows into 3-row border units. Make 2.

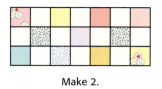

Make 2.

6. Fold the 9¼" muslin square in quarters to find its center; then crease the block on both diagonals. These fold lines will assist you later in placing the appliqué design on the block.

7. Sew a unit from step 5 to each side of the 9¼" muslin square. Press seams toward the pieced border unit.

8. Sew a border unit from step 3 to the top and bottom, carefully matching seamlines. Press.

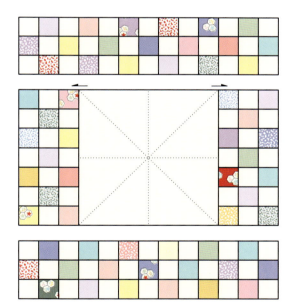

Appliquéing the Center Block

1. Use the patterns on page 73 to make templates for pieces A–F. Trace the templates and cut 2 A pieces and 1 C piece from the red and pink scraps, 2 B pieces and 1 D piece from the yellow scraps, 3 E pieces from the green scraps, and 1 F piece from the 6" brown print square. Add a scant ¼" seam allowance to each fabric shape.

2. Cut a total of 3 bias strips, each ⅞" x 5½", from the green scraps.

3. Refer to the appliqué placement diagram on page 72 and the photo on page 69. Pin the 3 bias stems and appliqué pieces A–F in place on the creased muslin background square. Appliqué the stems and then the flower and pot appliqués in alphabetical order to the background. Be sure the flowers and the flower pot cover the short raw edges of the bias stems.

4. Use the tan/black stripe and light tan scraps to make 1 bee. Appliqué the bee in place.

Assembling the Pillow

1. Center the pillow top over the 17" square of batting; baste.

2. Hand or machine quilt as desired.

3. Place the 10⅞" x 16¾" backing pieces wrong side up. Position a 2" x 16¾" piece of interfacing ¼" from and parallel to the long edge of each backing piece.

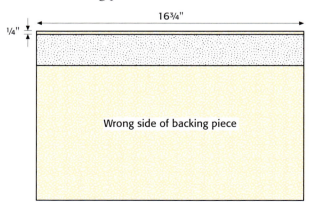

4. Fold the ¼" extension of backing toward the interfacing to make a hem on each backing piece. Machine stitch in place. Fold the edge again to make a 2" hem and topstitch in place. The 2" hem should completely cover the interfacing.

5. Referring to the diagram below for placement, make three 1" buttonholes along the interfaced edge of 1 backing piece.

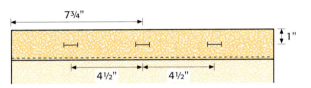

6. Place both backing pieces right side up, overlapping them so that the interfaced strips are on top of each other. The backing piece with the buttonholes should be on top. Pin the backing pieces at the overlapped hems, in between the buttonholes.

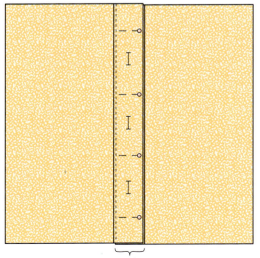

Overlap

7. Using the buttonholes as a guide, sew the 1" buttons in place and button them.

8. Place the completed pillow top and the completed, buttoned backing piece right sides together with raw edges aligned. Stitch a ¼" seam all around the outside.

9. Unbutton the backing and turn the pillow cover right side out. Stuff with a 16" pillow form. Button the pillow cover to finish.

Appliqué placement diagram

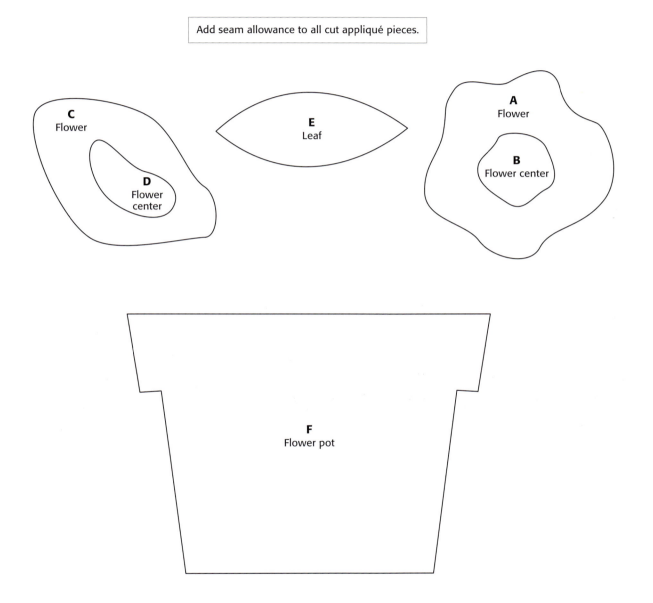

Add seam allowance to all cut appliqué pieces.

C
Flower

D
Flower
center

E
Leaf

A
Flower

B
Flower center

F
Flower pot

Good Morning Pillow

GOOD MORNING PILLOW by Linda Johnson, 1999, Auburn, Washington, 11" x 15".

FINISHED SIZE: 11" x 15"

Materials

42"-wide fabric

- ⅝ yd. muslin for appliqué background and pillow form
- Assorted scraps of '30s reproduction prints for flower appliqués and log cabin–style border
- Assorted green scraps for leaf appliqués
- Two 6" x 6" squares of blue prints for bird appliqué
- Assorted yellow print scraps for sun and sun ray appliqués
- Tan/black stripe scrap for bee appliqué
- Light tan scrap for bee wing appliqués
- Fat quarter yd. fabric for backing
- Architect's plastic ellipse template
- Erasable marker
- No. 5 perle cotton thread: green
- Skein of black embroidery floss
- 2 pieces of lightweight interfacing, each 1¾" x 11½"
- 3 buttons, 1" diameter
- 1 package of stuffing

Cutting

All cutting measurements include ¼"-wide seam allowances.

From the muslin, cut:
- 1 piece, 6½" x 10½", for appliqué background
- 2 pieces, each 11½" x 15½", for pillow form

From the assorted reproduction prints, cut a *total* of:
- 1 strip, 1¾" x 10½"
- 1 strip, 3" x 10½"
- 2 strips, each 1½" x 10¼"
- 2 strips, each 2 x 10¼"
- 1 strip, 1¾" x 15½"

(all for log cabin–style border)

From the backing fabric, cut:
- 2 pieces, each 10¼" x 12", for backing

Note: *Refer to "General Instructions" (pages 6–18) as needed for guidance with basic construction techniques.*

Appliquéing and Assembling the Pillow Top

1. Fold the 6½" x 10½" muslin background piece in quarters to find its center. These fold lines will assist you in placing the appliqué design on the background block.

2. Use the patterns on page 78 to make templates for pieces A–I. Trace the templates and cut 7 A pieces, 1 B piece, 1 C piece, and 3 H pieces from assorted yellow scraps; 1 each of pieces D and E from blue scraps; 1 F piece and

2 G pieces from reproduction scraps; and 4 I pieces from green scraps. Add a scant ¼" seam allowance to each fabric shape.

3. Refer to the diagram below. Center the sun template (B) approximately ¼" from the bottom raw edge of the 6½" x 10½" muslin background piece. Use an erasable marker to trace the sun's curve. Use this marking as a guideline for pinning piece B to the background block.

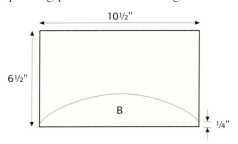

4. Referring to the diagram below, tuck the 7 A pieces behind the curve of the sun. The outside rays will extend beyond the end of the block.

5. Appliqué the sun rays and then the sun to the background block. Trim the outside sun rays even with the edges of the block.

6. Refer to the assembly diagram below. Sew the 1¾" x 10½" strip to the top edge of the muslin block. Press seams toward the strip. Continue adding strips in alphabetical order, following the sequence indicated on the assembly diagram. Press each strip as it is added.

7. Referring to the appliqué placement diagram on page 77, lay out and pin appliqué pieces C–I to the bordered block. Appliqué the pieces in alphabetical order to the block.

8. Use a single strand of No. 5 green perle cotton thread and a backstitch to embroider the stems beneath the flowers. Use a single strand of black embroidery floss and a backstitch to embroider the bird's feet and worm. Use the black embroidery floss to make a French-knot bird's eye.

9. Use the lettering on page 78 and an erasable marker to trace the words "Good Morning" onto the appliquéd pillow top. Use a single strand of embroidery floss and a backstitch to embroider the words.

10. Use the tan/black stripe and light tan scraps to make 1 bee. Appliqué the bee in place as shown on the placement diagram.

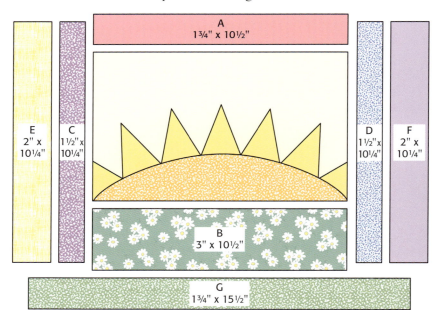

Assembly diagram
Measurements shown are *cut* sizes.

Assembling the Pillow

1. Follow steps 1 though 8 on pages 71–72 to baste, quilt, and assemble the pillow cover, substituting the appropriately sized batting, backing pieces, and interfacing. The diagram below indicates placement for the 3 buttonholes.

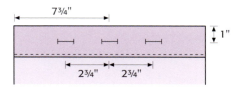

2. Make a pillow form by placing the 11½" x 15½" muslin pieces right sides together, and stitching a ¼" seam all around the outside edge. Leave a 5" opening in one side.

3. Turn the pillow form right side out and stuff generously. Hand stitch the opening closed.

4. Unbutton the pillow cover and turn it right side out. Insert the pillow form and button the pillow cover to finish.

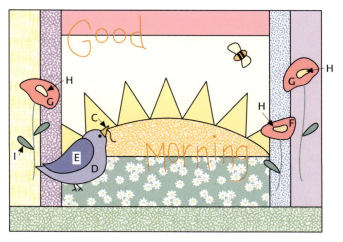

Appliqué placement diagram

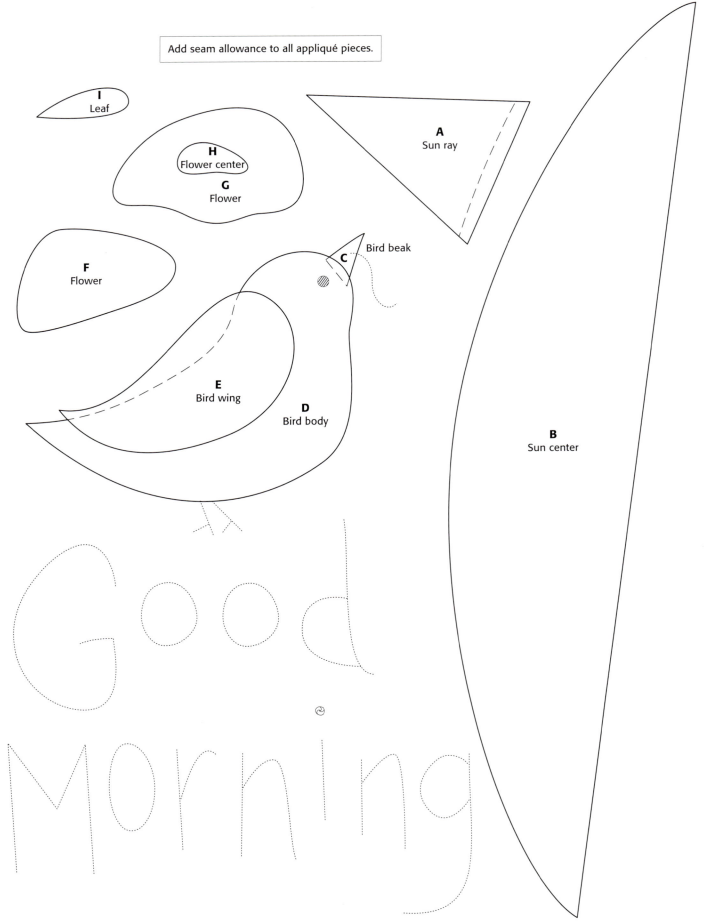

Add seam allowance to all appliqué pieces.

I
Leaf

H
Flower center

G
Flower

A
Sun ray

F
Flower

C
Bird beak

E
Bird wing

D
Bird body

B
Sun center

About the Author

LINDA JOHNSON was born in San Jose, California, and attended San Jose State College as a design major and home economics minor. She has been married for thirty-one years and has three children: a son in college and two daughters in high school. She and her family live in an old farmhouse outside Auburn, Washington, with three cats, ten chickens, and six sewing machines. Sewing has been a passion of Linda's since she was nine years old, and she has been quilting off and on for twenty-five years. She currently works at Calico Cat & Bernina Too in Auburn.

NEW AND BESTSELLING TITLES FROM

America's Best-Loved Craft & Hobby Books™

America's Best-Loved Quilt Books®

QUILTING
from That Patchwork Place, an imprint of Martingale & Company

Appliqué
Artful Appliqué
Colonial Appliqué
Red and Green: An Appliqué Tradition
Rose Sampler Supreme
Your Family Heritage: Projects in
   Appliqué

Baby Quilts
Appliqué for Baby
The Quilted Nursery
Quilts for Baby: Easy as ABC
More Quilts for Baby: Easy as ABC
Even More Quilts for Baby: Easy as ABC

Holiday Quilts
Easy and Fun Christmas Quilts
Favorite Christmas Quilts from That
   Patchwork Place
Paper Piece a Merry Christmas
A Snowman's Family Album Quilt
Welcome to the North Pole

Learning to Quilt
Basic Quiltmaking Techniques for:
   Borders and Bindings
   Curved Piecing
   Divided Circles
   Eight-Pointed Stars
   Hand Appliqué
   Machine Appliqué
   Strip Piecing
The Joy of Quilting
The Quilter's Handbook
Your First Quilt Book (or it should be!)

Paper Piecing
50 Fabulous Paper-Pieced Stars
A Quilter's Ark
Easy Machine Paper Piecing
Needles and Notions
Paper-Pieced Curves
Show Me How to Paper Piece

Rotary Cutting
101 Fabulous Rotary-Cut Quilts
365 Quilt Blocks a Year Perpetual
   Calendar
Fat Quarter Quilts
Lap Quilting Lives!
Quick Watercolor Quilts
Quilts from Aunt Amy
Spectacular Scraps
Time-Crunch Quilts

Small & Miniature Quilts
Bunnies By The Bay Meets Little Quilts
Celebrate! with Little Quilts
Easy Paper-Pieced Miniatures
Little Quilts All Through the House

CRAFTS
From Martingale & Company

300 Papermaking Recipes
The Art of Handmade Paper and
   Collage
The Art of Stenciling
Creepy Crafty Halloween
Gorgeous Paper Gifts
Grow Your Own Paper
Stamp with Style
Wedding Ribbonry

KNITTING
From Martingale & Company

Comforts of Home
Fair Isle Sweaters Simplified
Knit It Your Way
Simply Beautiful Sweaters
Two Sticks and a String
The Ultimate Knitter's Guide
Welcome Home: Kaffe Fassett

COLLECTOR'S COMPASS™
From Martingale & Company

20th Century Glass
'50s Decor
Barbie® Doll
Jewelry

Coming to *Collector's Compass* Spring 2001:

20th Century Dinnerware
American Coins
Movie Star Collectibles
'60s Decor

Our books are available at bookstores and your favorite craft, fabric, yarn, and antiques retailers. If you don't see the title you're looking for, visit us at **www.martingale-pub.com** or contact us at:

1-800-426-3126
International: 1-425-483-3313
Fax: 1-425-486-7596
E-mail: info@martingale-pub.com

For more information and a full list of our titles, visit our Web site or call for a free catalog.